SIMPLE SPELLS WITH PLAYING CARDS
BY
Maria D'Andrea

SIMPLE SPELLS WITH PLAYING CARDS
by
Maria D'Andrea
Introduction by Sean Casteel

This edition Copyright © 2015 by Global Communications/Conspiracy Journal

All rights reserved. No part of these manuscripts may be copied or reproduced by any mechanical or digital methods and no exerpts or quotes may be used in any other book or manuscript without permission in writing by the Publisher, Global Communications/Conspiracy Journal, except by a reviewer who may quote brief passages in a review.

Revised Edition

Published in the United States of America By
Global Communications/Conspiracy Journal
Box 753 · New Brunswick, NJ 08903

Staff Members
Timothy G. Beckley, Publisher
Carol Ann Rodriguez, Assistant to the Publisher
Sean Casteel, General Associate Editor
Tim R. Swartz, Graphics and Editorial Consultant
William Kern, Editorial and Art Consultant

Sign Up On The Web For Our Free Weekly Newsletter
and Mail Order Version of Conspiracy Journal
and Bizarre Bazaar
www.ConspiracyJournal.com

**Order Hot Line: 1-732-602-3407
PayPal: MrUFO8@hotmail.com**

Maria D'Andrea's Simple Spells With Playing Cards

**TELLING FORTUNES AND CASTING SPELLS
WITH PLAYING CARDS**

By Sean Casteel

The origin of playing cards and their use in divination is shrouded in the mists of time.

But Maria D'Andrea offers an alternative to any previous fatalistic interpretations by teaching the reader to use ordinary playing cards to cast helpful spells and thus gain a measure of control over your life circumstances.

D'Andrea lays out a series of spells that are intended to attract love and friendship into your life or to give you a more balanced outlook in your daily struggle to survive and flourish in healthy ways. With step-by-step instructions, she leads you through a simple process that combines the burning of certain colored candles and incense with the laying out of carefully chosen cards. You can then connect with various "higher powers" while maintaining your personal dignity and free will.

If you tend to think of casting spells as kind of a "witchy" endeavor, D'Andrea is quick to point out that the use of cards in divination comes down to us from ancient times and was not considered either positive or negative in and of itself. She also reassures us that occultism really consists of understanding the Laws of Nature and how to work with them. Occultism is the oldest science in the world, she writes, and was the starting point for many of today's commonly accepted "hard" sciences – such as modern chemistry and its origins in alchemy.

One of the spells D'Andrea provides is a "Ritual For Banishing Negativity In Your Home." The ritual requires the ace of spades, the five of diamonds, and the ace of hearts. One also needs two candles, one light blue and the other yellow. Next, three drops of pine or frankincense oil and one cup or more of vinegar.

Maria D'Andrea's Simple Spells With Playing Cards

Once you have laid out the cards and followed up on the other simple steps, you reach out to the divine powers by saying the required words of the ritual three times. Then you basically sit back and await the results, which could come in any number of ways, so be observant of how people and situations start to work themselves out in more positive ways around your home.

GIVING THE DARKNESS FAIR WARNING

D'Andrea advises you to say her "Quick Protection Prayer" before beginning your exploration of playing cards, spells and rituals. You must make it clear to whatever forces or entities are at work that you don't intend to voluntarily end up in some matrix of evil or to harm yourself or anyone else. Without your complicity, the dark side of the spirit world can't exert any sort of unhealthy grip on your life.

"In simple terms," D'Andrea writes, "the practitioner is the one who is positive or negative and decides how he or she will work with the tools before them. I only do positive work because I truly believe what you put out comes back to you – good/bad/or indifferently. We utilize various tools to manifest creating a better life. Tarot, and, more recently, playing cards are one of the older systems and have been utilized by shamans, magi, occultists, parapsychologists, spiritual workers – to name only a few of these types of practitioners."

And while Maria takes a decisively occult approach to the cards, several scholars in the field of Cartomancy confirm that "reading cards" per se has been practiced for centuries.

PLAYING CARDS ARE NOT MERELY FOR GAMES

"In our day and generation," classic occult author Carleton B. Case writes, "divination by cards is chiefly employed for amusement and pastime, for the entertainment of one's self or one's company, or at church fairs, charity bazaars, and the like; but in the days of the ancients it was practiced by prophets and sibyls as a serious business, and so accepted by all, from king to peasant."

Just when playing cards were first developed is often traced back to Italy in the 13th or 14th century, but the details remain lost to history. Our present-day deck of 52 cards is said to be the offspring of the 78 cards of the tarot deck, which were originally used for card games as well as for telling the future. But as to which appeared on the scene of human affairs first, there is much disagreement among historians and card enthusiasts. Besides the Italians, some credit the French or the Chinese, while others see the hand of ancient Egypt at work in some of the symbolism the cards embody.

Case summarizes his own work as "a gathering together in handy form of

Maria D'Andrea's Simple Spells With Playing Cards

the best authenticated methods of its ancient practice as handed down from the Romany gypsies and the seeresses that antedate them." Which conjures the typical image we often have when it comes to fortune-telling: an elderly gypsy crone laying out the cards while a young lovelorn woman waits in trembling expectation to learn what sort of romantic future she is fated to have.

SUPERNATURAL POWERS NOT REQUIRED

"Certainly there is a wonderful fascination in the mastering of Cartomancy," Case writes, "in the being able to tell fortunes by the chance falling of the cards into this or that position, and in knowing what each card and grouping is believed to signify in their relations to the person consulting.

"No prophet or seer ever professed that divination by cards is a natural gift," he continues. "It is universally recognized as being solely the result of study and practice, and can be mastered by anyone who has this book and gives the subject a little thought and sufficient experimental, practical testing to acquire proficiency." In other words, anyone who applies himself to the art can learn it. One needn't have been born with supernatural powers.

WHAT THOSE FAMILIAR CARDS ARE REALLY SAYING

According to Case, various meanings have been ascribed to individual cards in different countries and times. Certain suits and individual cards have their own personalities, as if they are a living entity. For example, clubs mostly portend happiness and good business arrangements, and no matter how they are combined with other suits, they are seldom considered as bearers of other than the best omens.

"Next come hearts," Case writes, "which are usually taken to signify lovemaking, invitations and good friends; diamonds, money; and spades, annoyances, sickness or worry, sometimes loss of money."

The king of clubs represents a man who is humane, upright, and affectionate; faithful in all his undertakings. He will be happy himself and make everyone around him so. The queen of clubs is a tender, mild and rather susceptible woman who will be very attractive to the opposite sex, while the jack of clubs is an open, sincere and good friend who will exert himself warmly in your welfare.

By contrast, the king of diamonds has a fiery temper, is continually angry and seeking revenge in his stubbornness. The king of hearts is good natured but rash in his undertakings and very amorous. In the spades, one finds darkness. For instance, the queen of spades is a woman who can be corrupted by the rich of both sexes and is frequently a widow. The nine of spades is professed to be the worst card of the pack; dangerous sickness, total loss of fortune and calamities;

Maria D'Andrea's Simple Spells With Playing Cards

also endless dissension in your family.

When you apply this sort of understanding to a simple deck of 52 playing cards, one finds material for a soap opera or even an epic miniseries.

MAN IS A GAMBLING ANIMAL

To quote another scholarly approach to the history and meaning of cards, there is "Facts and Speculations on the Origin and History of Playing Cards," by William Andrew Chatto. Chatto also grapples with the various historical accounts of when, where and how playing cards originated and admits there is no easy way to chart their development based on the records now available.

But Chatto also notes, rather philosophically, that man – alone in all the animal kingdom – is a "gambler," willing to surrender his life circumstances to games of chance or risking his future to a set of cards "randomly" dealt by a seer or fortune teller. The possible dark outcome portended by the laying out of cards cannot be easily averted and the risk is very real that fate will play itself out according to the whims of whatever force is guiding the mysterious art of Cartomancy.

But one doesn't have to passively accept the fortune meted out by the seemingly random way the cards fall. Maria has adapted the lessons of the ages and has added her own spin – using candles, incense and the recitation of words that can make the "higher powers" do your bidding through the cards. You are, Maria says, in control of your future with her methods and are not subject to the whims of unseen forces working through artful pieces of cardboard. This is a golden opportunity to gaze into and control the future from a perspective of self-determination.

After reading this book and utilizing the tools laid out for you, a new adventure with playing cards will await you every time you shuffle a deck.

Saturday night poker with the boys will never be the same!

Maria D'Andrea's Simple Spells With Playing Cards

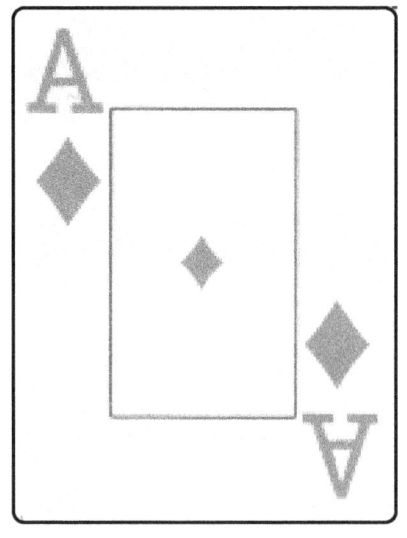

SHUFFLE THE CARDS FOR LUCK, LOVE

AND PROSPERITY

Fabulous Fortunes Can Be Yours By Reading An Ordinary Deck Of Playing Cards

Maria D'Andrea, Ms.D, D.D., D.R.H.

From time immemorial, an ordinary deck of playing cards has been utilized successfully to venture into the future and gain insights into a person's life. As an oracle, these cards can assist you in making better decisions regarding your living conditions and help avoid negative situations that can pop up on a day to day basis.

The deck of 52 playing cards, which we play games of chance with today, originated from the very ancient Tarot decks, which were also used in occult practices. Their meanings were cloaked in secret ancient wisdom and hidden knowledge. They were not considered positive or negative on their own and were not tied in with any religion. The occult (also called metaphysics or parapsychology, among other terms), simply put, is understanding of the Laws of Nature and how one can learn to work with them. The occult is the oldest science in the world. For instance, we know that the "hard" science of chemistry emerged from the earlier occult science of alchemy.

In simple terms, the practitioner is the one who is positive or negative and decides how he or she will work with the tools before them. I only do positive work because I truly believe what you put out comes back to you – good/bad/or indifferently.

Maria D'Andrea's Simple Spells With Playing Cards

We utilize various tools to manifest creating a better life. Tarot and, more recently, playing cards are one of the older systems and have been utilized by shamans, magi, occultists, parapsychologists, spiritual workers – to name only a few of these types of practitioners.

Prior to the cards, there were various symbols drawn on wood, stone and other objects. Many of these unique systems are still utilized today.

Spells/formulae have been passed down for generations, Master to Initiate and parent to child. The power and force behind this ability was not shared easily, especially because putting the knowledge in the wrong (negative) hands can be devastating.

This is not a game and you need to be serious about doing ONLY positive work. Meaning that, when you improve your life, it causes no harm nor exerts any negative control over others and their free will. Remember, what you do will come back. Accordingly, there is "The Law of Threefold." This states that what you send out to the Universe comes back threefold to you. That is something that must be considered when you contemplate doing something that can only reverberate with negative repercussions.

Starting On Your Path

Most people are unaware of how these energies of the Universe work. You are tapping into a source of nature and need to be sure that you are safe. I always teach utilizing psychic self-defense first to all my international students and the ones I teach here because you absolutely need to be safe.

I also mention Protection in my numerous other books, TV shows, radio, public speaking/lecturing/workshops, among my other venues. It is a priority.

One easily used method is to do a prayer specifically for this purpose.

You need only to repeat my "Quick Protection Prayer" seriously, from the heart, and with positive intent. Saying it out loud gives it more power but it also works if you mentally say it.

Maria's Quick Protection Prayer

Through earth and sky,

Through fire and rain,

With focused heart,

I now do pray.

*

Maria D'Andrea's Simple Spells With Playing Cards

Divine Power of Infinite Love,

Protect me now from ALL that harms.

*

So Be It. Thank You.

Make sure you are clear about what you are manifesting before you begin. When you start after the prayer, be sure to stay focused on your goal the whole time and allow yourself to also add your feelings about the situation you are working on.

After all, if you don't have any feelings about it, the Universe will not either. Your feelings are that battery charger.

As an example: If you have a good car, but would like to have a newer one at some point, your feelings reflect it and you are not in a rush or anxious. You will get there when you get there. However, say you have a car that you need to get to work each day and all of a sudden your car breaks down and can't be repaired. Think of how you would feel. You would be upset, anxious, and you would be very focused on the fact that you have to get a car immediately. These are very different levels of feelings. Your focus when you are manifesting needs to be the second type to charge it with the correct energy. A little like powering up your energy.

Next :

It is also very important to have a feeling of expectancy. If you ask a friend to pick up some milk for you when she is at the store and she agrees, you know she will bring it. You may not know exactly when she will be at your home, but you know she is coming with what you asked for. You expect her. This is the same principle. You know what you are manifesting is coming, so keep an eye out for it.

Get your cards:

You will need a playing deck of any type that you are drawn to. It doesn't matter if it can be read upside down or not for spells/formulae.

Take three days to place your deck in direct sunlight to release any negative energy it might be holding, such as a disgruntled warehouse worker who handled it or any other negative energy that may be attached. For direct sunlight, you can place the deck on a windowsill, a kitchen table that gets sunlight, or anywhere that is convenient for you.

Now, you are ready to start.

Maria D'Andrea's Simple Spells With Playing Cards

Note: The cards for occult/spell use do not necessarily match the meaning for reading the cards.

Money Success

This formula attracts money or money opportunities to you. Pay attention to what is going on around you once you have finished this formula so you do not miss the opportunities that come.

Look for the following cards in the deck, take them out, and place them to the side.

Ace of Diamonds

Five of Clubs

Six of Clubs

Focus on your intent, with seriousness and emotional feeling, as you lay the cards out in a place you can leave them, such as a drawer or dresser top, etc., in the following way, face up:

PLACEMENT:

1st card – Ace of Diamonds – place on the left.

2nd card – Five of Clubs – place next to the 1st card on the right.

3rd card – Six of Clubs – place on top of both cards in the center so it forms a peak.

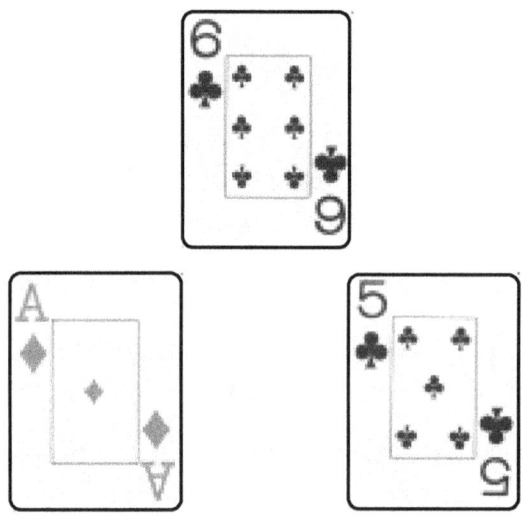

3

1 2

Maria D'Andrea's Simple Spells With Playing Cards

PROCEDURE:

Leave the cards there until your money or opportunity manifests.

The outcome may come in a variety of forms. It could be through business, a relationship, luck or several other ways. Remember, when an opportunity develops that you do not have to take it. As an example: When you have a chance to take a new job or to move up in your current one but you don't want to because it's not something you think you will like. After all, we all have free will.

In that case, shuffle the cards, find the three cards utilized in this spell and redo the spell the same way as before.

For ALL Card Spells in which only cards are used

You can also take a picture of this or any other layout once you are finished and carry the picture with you in your wallet, pocketbook or wherever you would like.

Balance Your Spirit, Mind and Body

Incense has been incorporated in magickal rites and to connect to deities since ancient times. Today, you can add it to this spell to heighten your connection to higher, positive, spiritual help in gaining balance in your life.

The scent has the ability on a vibrational level to attract your intent. The name of the incense for this situation is Rose Incense.

This formula with the cards will help you to elevate to a higher balance within yourself. The cards will help you to promote the outcome you are creating faster.

Focus on your intent to have balance in your body, mind and spirit. "See" yourself calm, happy, well and, in general, balanced already.

Take three slow, deep breaths and then shuffle the cards with your focused intent.

Take out the following six cards and set them aside:

Ace of Hearts

Ace of Spades

Nine of Hearts

Ten of Hearts

Ten of Spades

Three of Hearts

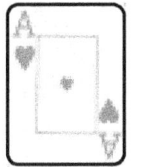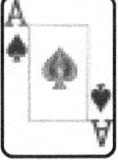

Maria D'Andrea's Simple Spells With Playing Cards

Get the stone called Hematite. This will add to your ability to maintain this balance.

Add a white Candle of any size.

Have about two to three Tablespoons of Sea or Kosher salt.

Now you are ready to proceed with the spell.

You are forming a square with the card layout in the center.

PLACEMENT – With Focus:

1 – Place the Hematite stone directly in front of you while leaving enough space to place your cards between the stone and the white Candle.

2 – Place the White Candle directly in front of you

3 – Place the Rose Incense to your right.

4 – Place the Sea Salt to your left.

5 – Still with intent, place the cards in the middle in this order:

From left to right, next to each other in a row, touching –

(1) Ace of Hearts, (2) Ace of Spades, (3) Nine of Hearts, (4) Ten of Hearts, (5) Ten of Spades, (6) Three of Hearts

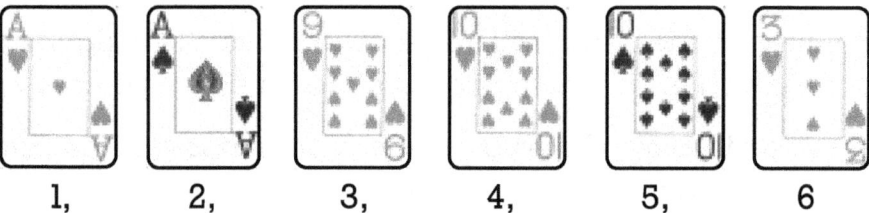

1, 2, 3, 4, 5, 6

PROCEDURE:

1 – Light the Rose Incense.

2 – Light the White Candle.

3 – Looking at the cards, with reverence and sincerity, recite 3 times:

Divine Power surround (<u>name of person or say "me"</u>),

    Bring balance into my life,

    May strength, love and truth overpower all obstacles,

    May peace reign over my life.

Maria D'Andrea's Simple Spells With Playing Cards

So Might It Be.

4 – You can now let the Incense and Candle burn to the bottom.

5 – When it is all done, place the cards back in the deck or leave them out as they are.

6 – Take the Sea Salt, the remains of the Incense and Candle and throw them away outside your home.

7 – Carry the stone with you. Know that your balance is now regained.

Ritual For Banishing Negativity In Your Home

At times, there is negative energy in the home. You don't need to live with this energy that slows you down, upsets you and drains you.

TOOLS:

The following cards are to be put aside for this ritual:

Ace of Spades

Five of Diamonds

Ace of Hearts

 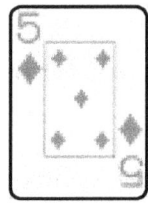 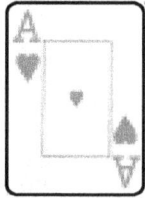

The two candles to be used: Light Blue and Yellow (any size).

Three drops of Pine or Frankincense Oil.

One cup or more of Vinegar

PLACEMENT:

1 – Place the cards in an arc shape from left to right in this order in the center of your room:

(1) Ace of Spades, (2) Five of Diamonds, (3) Ace of Hearts on top.

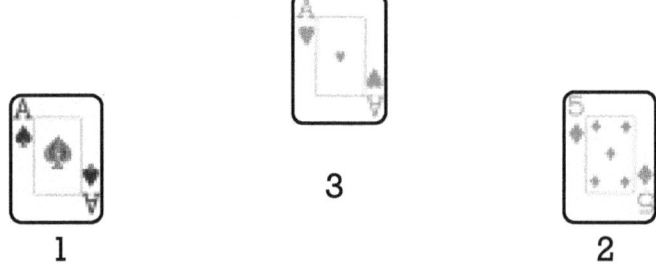

Maria D'Andrea's Simple Spells With Playing Cards

2 – Place three drops of the Pine or Frankincense Oil on top of each candle.

3 – Place the Blue Candle on the left of the cards and the Yellow Candle on the right.

4 – Take the vinegar and place it directly in front of you.

PROCEDURE:

1 – Focus your intent on creating a positive, happy, safe environment.

2 – Repeat the following three times with conviction as a command:

Through Divine Power and in a positive way,

All that is negative and in <u>(my or name of person)</u> way now banishes back to whence it came,

All that is pure and of the Light now envelopes darkness and takes it out of sight,

And as I say so shall it be.

3 – At this time, pick up the vinegar and walk away to let the candles burn out to the bottom.

4 – Sprinkle the vinegar in each corner of each room.

5 – When the candles are finished, throw them away outside your home.

6 – Pick up the cards in reverse order, right to left, and place them back in the deck.

Remember to keep positive, happy thoughts in your mind daily. After all, if you are safe, you are happy.

Maria D'Andrea's Simple Spells With Playing Cards

Love/Friendship Comes to Me

This card spell attracts love and/or friendship. This means your focus has to be on which one or both at all times during the spell casting.

Do not focus on a specific person or name. If you are meant to be together in a positive way, then it will happen. If it is not a positive situation for one or both of you, then someone else will come along that you will be happy with.

As an example: I had a client who came to me for several years for readings. She asked me to help her to get married to a specific gentleman. I declined, explaining that it "felt off" to me. So she went to someone else who worked on what she wanted. They were eventually married. A few years later, before we began to do a reading, she started to cry. She explained that soon after she was married, he became violent and now she had to leave him. He only became like that after marriage because he grew up with his father being violent with his mother. He wasn't even aware he had that tendency until after marriage. If you "call in" a situation spiritually, it is harder to cancel it.

Once you are finished with the spell, you need to look for and expect the person to come along. Your emotions will charge the situation and become a magnet to attract the person to you.

START this formula on a Friday:

Take out the following cards from your deck:

Two of Hearts

Three of Hearts

Five of Diamonds

Four of Clubs

Ace of Hearts

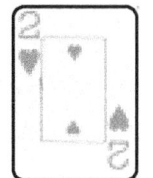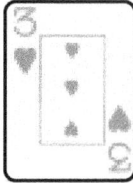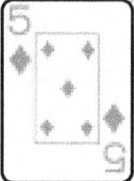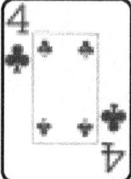

Make a photocopy of them and use the photocopies.

Get the pink stone called Rhodocrosite or Rhodonite. Also good are the stones called Moonstone or Turquoise. Pick one of these to work with.

The following herbs are used: Rose, Rosemary or Thyme.

A cup filled with some water is also needed.

Do the FOLLOWING:

1 – Place the cup containing the water to your left.

Maria D'Andrea's Simple Spells With Playing Cards

2 – The herb (you can use one or more) gets sprinkled into the water.

3 – Next, place the photocopies of the cards in the following manner:

Starting on your right side, place the (1) Two of Hearts, then next to it the (2) Three of Hearts.

Leave a little space and place the (3) Five of Diamonds.

Once again, leave a little space and place the (4) Four of Clubs, then the (5) Ace of Hearts.

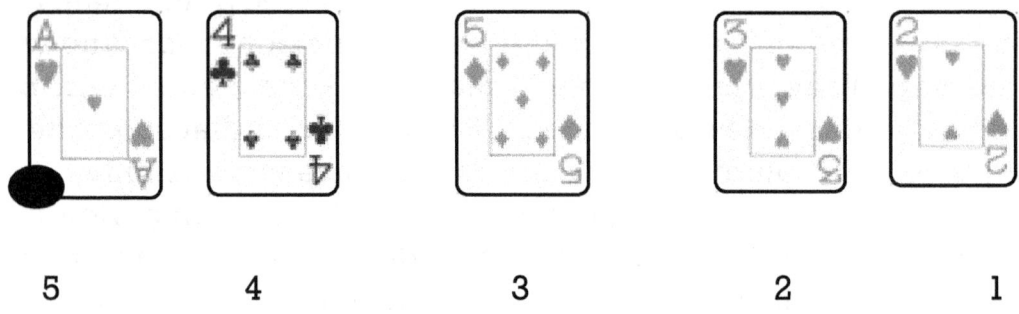

    5   4   3   2   1

4 – Place your choice of stone upon the last card, the Ace of Hearts.

5 – Focus now on your intent and command verbally from the heart:

I now conjure thus, for the benefit of all involved,

I attract <u>(love and/or friendship)</u> into my life,

To improve our lives, joy, harmony and with love,

As I speak this truth, it now goes to the ethers and comes back to the physical to manifest.

I declare it to be so, and so it is.

6 — Rinse your hands with the water. Put three drops on your heart. Then sprinkle a little of the water at your entryway. If there is any left, throw it away outside your home.

7 – Take the photocopies and pick them up in the same order you put them down. Make them into one pile and place them under your bed or mattress.

Maria D'Andrea's Simple Spells With Playing Cards

8 – Take the stone and carry it with you at all times.

Remember to be loving, smile and be happy. There is an occult law that states "Like attracts like." Have fun.

Speed Up Spell For Health

The way all healing works is by speeding up your natural healing process.

To speed things up, do the following

TOOLS:

The stone named Red Jasper

The following cards: (1) Four of Spades, (2) Ace of Clubs, (3) Three of Cups

Draw in black ink on white paper the alchemy symbol for the ether: **"O"**

Take two candles (of any size) 1st a Pink Candle and 2nd a Green Candle.

Do the following:

Wear something green (can be a scarf, handkerchief, shirt, etc.) while performing this spell.

ACTIVATION:

1 – Draw the alchemy symbol on a paper large enough to place the cards on.

2 – Place the cards from right to left, as if they were a stairway, inside the alchemy symbol.

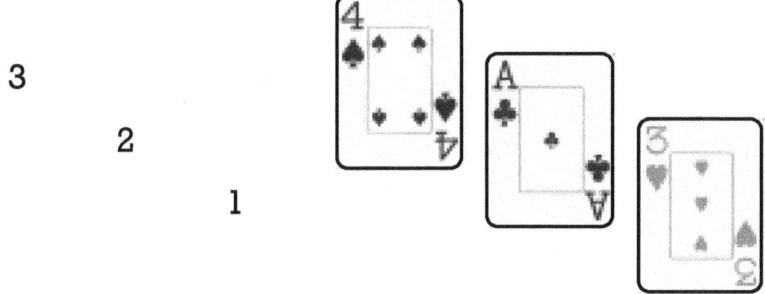

Maria D'Andrea's Simple Spells With Playing Cards

3 – Take the red Jasper and place it on the center card. (2)

4 – Place the Pink Candle on the left of the paper and the Green Candle on the right of the paper. Light the candles right to left with intent, focus and emotion.

5 – Now activate this intent with power.

6 – With intent, "see" yourself on the first (card) step being better then you are. Then, on the next step, still better than before. And on the last step, where you are a healthy body with a happy spirit. "See" yourself doing active, happy adventures. Pay attention to how you would feel in that situation.

7 – Speak the following Words of Power as a command:

East, West, North and South, I command your Energies of Healing to enfold me, surround me and permeate through me with your Blessed Light. I call forth the Protecting, Positive Healing Masters from all directions to come to me and stay with me until my intent is achieved.

Thank you for our aid. So Be It.

8 – Pick up the stone to carry with you always. Keep it within three feet of your body.

9 – Place the cards back in your deck.

10 – Allow the candles to burn to the bottom and then throw them away outside your home.

11— Take the paper with the alchemy symbol and burn it until it is all ashes. Relight the paper if you need to. When it is all ashes, take the ashes outside and throw them to the wind.

Maria D'Andrea's Simple Spells With Playing Cards

Wish Attraction

Wish attraction spells heighten your chances of gaining or making your wishes manifest.

Make sure your wishes are positive and of benefit to you or someone else. It is always wise to be on the positive side. Think of how your wish will affect you and those around you and then, if you feel it's good, proceed.

TIME: Do this spell during the night, anytime between sunset and sunrise.

Your TOOLS will be:

      On white paper, with red ink, draw a triangle

      Some Lavender – dried or fresh, as long as it has the scent.

      The following cards: Seven of Clubs, Eight of Diamonds,

      Nine of Hearts, Six of Clubs, Ace of Hearts

Do the FOLLOWING with intent:

1 – Place the paper with the triangle in front of you, the point being at the top.

2 – Place the cards down in the following order, starting from the bottom and placing each card above the last: (1) Seven of Clubs, (2) Eight of Diamonds, (3) Nine of Hearts, (4) Six of Clubs, (5), Ace of Hearts.

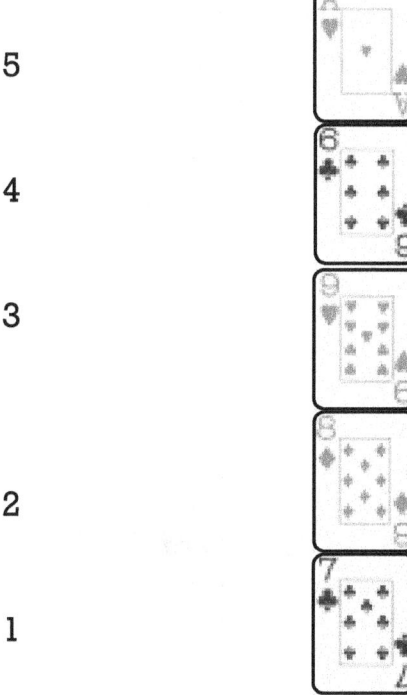

5

4

3

2

1

Maria D'Andrea's Simple Spells With Playing Cards

3 – Place the Lavender on top of the top (5th) card.

4 – Visualize a gigantic, happy Orange and Yellow Dragon.

5 – Repeat three times:

> Dragon, Dragon of the night,
>
> Awaken to make your spirit bright,
>
> Hear my wish (say your wish) and spread your wings,
>
> With ageless power my wish bring.
>
> And now go forth. SO BE IT!

6 – Take a few minutes to focus. Allow yourself to feel happy since your wish is coming to pass.

7 – Take the Lavender and sprinkle it near your bed.

8 – Take the cards and place them back in your deck.

9 – Burn the paper to ashes and throw away outside your home.

Happy Life

Part of happiness is our outlook on life. Even when things are not as they should be, there is always something we can find to be happy about. A positive past experience, a friend, or the sound of a song you like, among various other things, can create happy thoughts. Focus on happy things and you will heighten that feeling and it will become a habit.

This spell helps you to bring that feeling to you more quickly and helps you in not only attaining it, but keeping it going.

The FOLLOWING are needed:

Take out the cards known as: The Ace of Hearts, Two of Hearts, and Three of Hearts. Make a photocopy of them to work with.

A Yellow Candle – any size.

A piece of White or Yellow handkerchief or material to keep the cards in.

Maria D'Andrea's Simple Spells With Playing Cards

ACTIVATION:

1 – Place the cards from left to right: (1) Ace of Hearts, (2) Two of Hearts, (3), Three of Hearts.

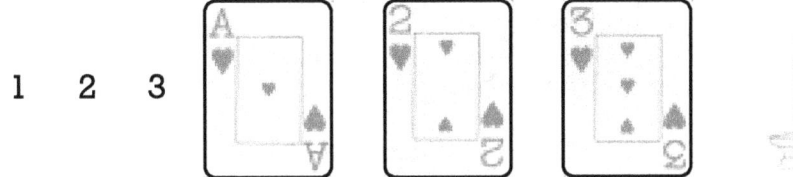

2 – Place the Yellow Candle to the right of the cards. While lighting it, focus on happy experiences, people you like, happy things in your life you can look forward to – like a day doing something that makes you happy. Any happy thoughts will do. Do this for a few minutes.

3 – Let the candle burn out. Throw the remains outside your home.

4 – Wrap the cards in the material. You can place the cards in your wallet or purse or somewhere in your room where you will see them every day, such as the top of a dresser.

5 – Keep them there until you feel happy. Then put them away somewhere you can easily get to whenever you feel you need them again.

Maria D'Andrea's Simple Spells With Playing Cards

Lucky Life

This will help you to increase your luck from whatever it is now. It heightens the vibrations to attract more luck and lucky situations.

Focus your thoughts on – I am always happy.

Keep an eye out for opportunities and get excited about what is coming up next for you.

Do "Maria's Quick Protection Prayer" or do your own. It is important to do so before starting to open the doors to the Universe.

Use the following <u>TOOLS</u>:

    Playing cards: Ace of Clubs, Ace of Hearts, Eight of Diamonds, Nine of Clubs and Ace of Diamonds.

    A piece of green material. Such as a small square cloth cut from green fabric. 3" x 3" would be best.

    The herb – Allspice or Nutmeg (this can be in powdered form or as the whole nut. Both can be found in your supermarket.)

ACTIVATION:

    1 – Place the following cards on the floor in a horseshoe shape, starting on the left top spot: (1) Ace of Clubs, (2) Ace of Hearts, (3) Eight of Diamonds, (4) Nine of Clubs, (5), Ace of Diamonds.

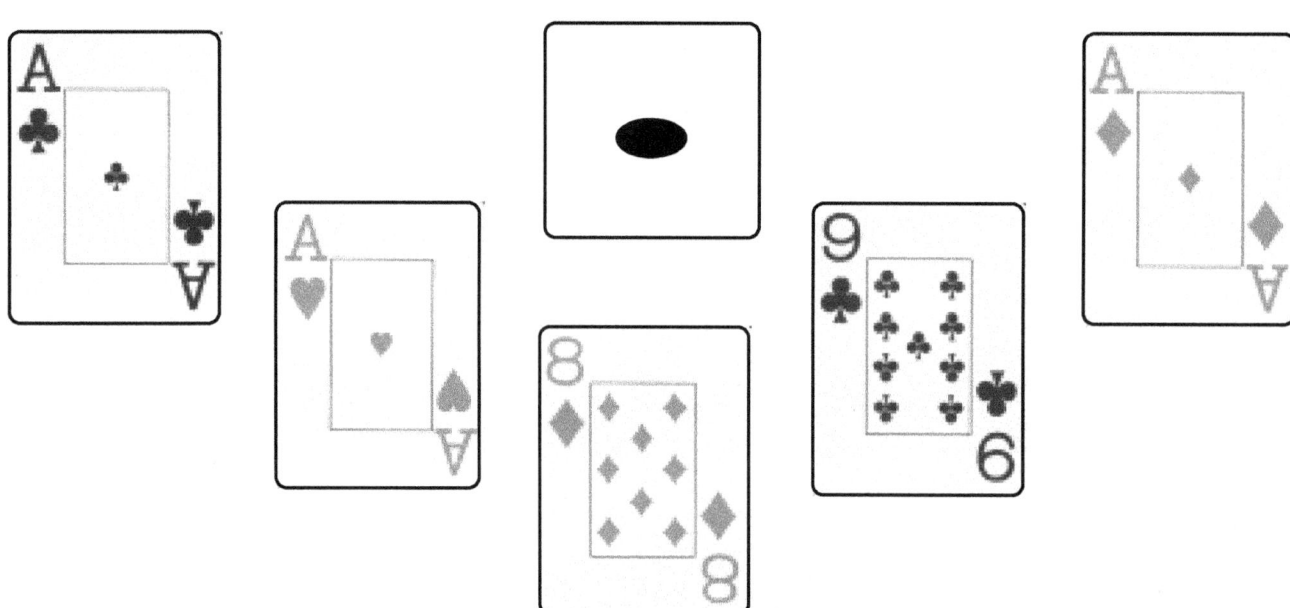

Maria D'Andrea's Simple Spells With Playing Cards

2 – Place the green material in the center.

3 – Place the Allspice or Nutmeg on the material.

4 – Be serious with your intent.

5 – Three times say, with conviction, focused intent, expectancy and joy:

Sand and stone,

Gems and gold,

I now call forth,

Luck to unfold.

And so it is.

6 – Take the green cloth and fold it with the herb in the center so you may carry it at all times.

7 – Take the cards up in reverse order from 5 to 1 and place back into the deck.

NOTE: You have to carry the cloth with the herb at all times to build up your magnetic field of energy. If you only carry it at times you feel you might need it, the vibration will not be as strong.

Maria D'Andrea's Simple Spells With Playing Cards

Light Work Meditation

Meditation is a powerful tool. It helps you to tune into intuitive information that can help you in making better decisions; gives you warnings; helps you to deal with a problem person in a better way; helps with your health and to stay calm, among other benefits.

Remember to do the Protection.

In this situation, if you simply sit in a comfortable position, on a chair, floor, or couch, it will give you the benefits.

You should disconnect phones and shut the TV, radio and other distractions off.

Place the following cards around you in a circle, starting at the top right hand corner from where you are sitting and face in the eastern direction: (1) Seven of Diamonds, (2) Seven of Hearts, (3) Seven of Clubs, (4) Seven of Spades, (5) Eight of Hearts, (6) Ace of Hearts, (7), Three of Clubs.

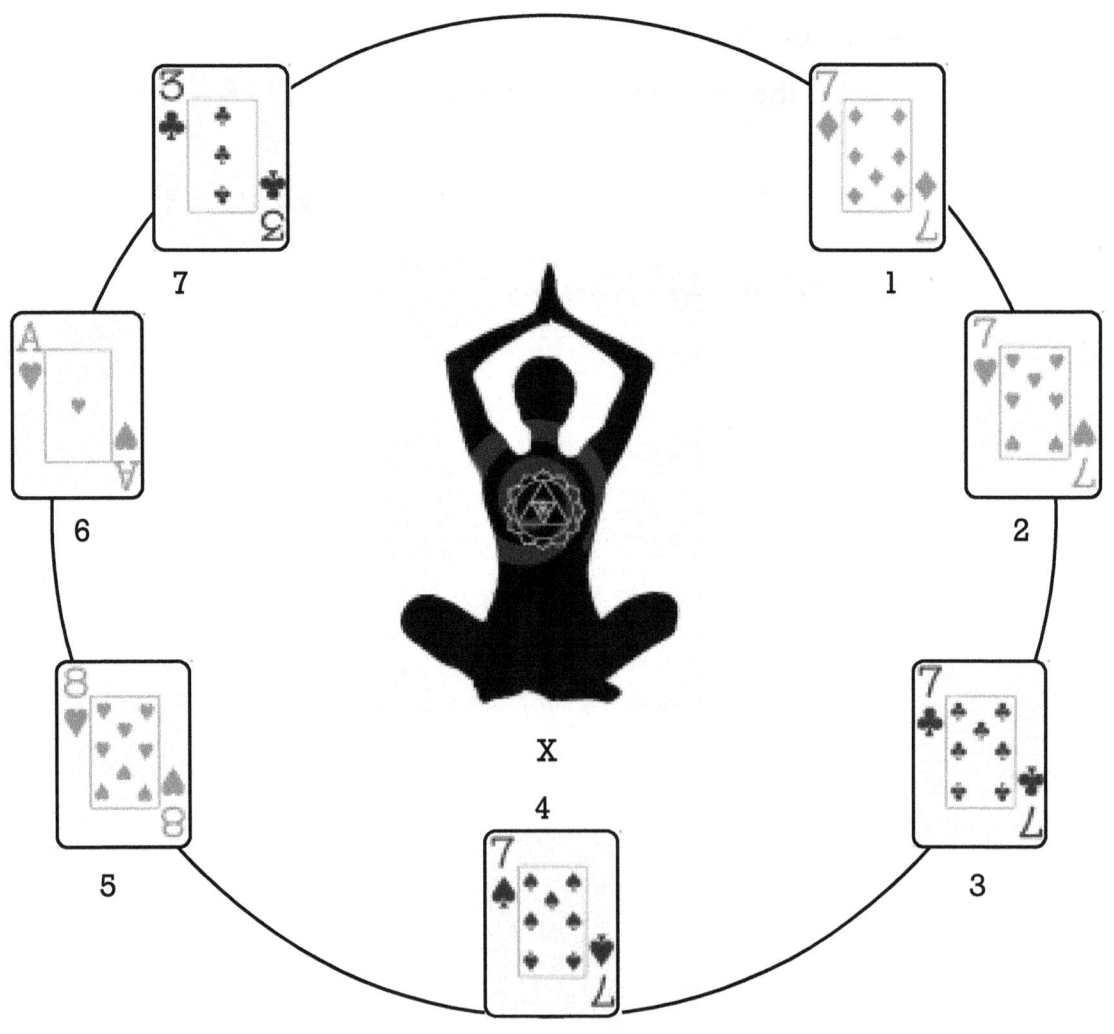

Maria D'Andrea's Simple Spells With Playing Cards

The X represents you sitting in the middle.

Sit in your place, close your eyes and make sure you feel comfortable. Relax and take three deep breaths, slowly. You can take more, but not less. Allow your mind to simply wander and pay attention to what you see, feel, sense or think.

You will have the urge on your own when it is time for you to stop. When you are finished, take one slow, deep breath and open your eyes.

Pick up the cards in reverse order, from 7 to 1. Place them back into your deck.

OPTION: You can photocopy these cards, place them together and save them for your next excursion into Light Work.

This will not be a mastering of intense meditation but it will give the ability to you to gain from the experience what you need to know or do.

Maria D'Andrea's Simple Spells With Playing Cards

Maria D'Andrea's Simple Spells With Playing Cards

TELLING FORTUNES BY CARDS

A SYMPOSIUM OF THE SEVERAL ANCIENT AND MODERN METHODS AS PRACTICED BY SIBYLS AND THE ROMANY GYPSIES, WITH PLAIN EXAMPLES AND SIMPLE INSTRUCTIONS TO ENABLE ANYONE TO ACQUIRE THE ART WITH EASE

Maria D'Andrea's Simple Spells With Playing Cards

CONTENTS

The Story of Josephine

Researching Gypsy Lore

How to Acquire the Art

Cards to be Used

The Consultant Card

The Ancient Oracle

Method A

Modern Use of Fifty-two Cards

Method B

Method C

Method D

Method E

Method F, the Star

Method G, a Shorter Star

Method H

Method I

Method J

Method K

Method L

Method M

The Preferred Oracle, with Thirty-two Cards

Dictionary of Primary Definitions

Dictionary of Secondary Definitions

Groups of Cards

Combinations of Two Cards

A Word of Advice

Special Note

Maria D'Andrea's Simple Spells With Playing Cards

Dealing the Cards by Threes

Dealing the Cards by Fives

Dealing the Cards by Sevens

Dealing by Fifteens

The Twenty-one Card Method

The Way to Tell a Fortune

The Italian Method

The Florence Mode

Past, Present and Future

The Matrimonial Oracle

The Star Method

Shorter Star Method

Wishes

Wish No. I.

Wish No. II.

Wish No. III.

Wish No. IV.

Wish No. V.

Wish No. VI.

Curious Games with Cards

Lovers' Hearts

Love's Lottery

Matrimony

Cupid's Pastime

Wedding Bells

Marriage Questions

Maria D'Andrea's Simple Spells With Playing Cards

TELLING FORTUNES BY CARDS

The art of telling fortunes by cards, known professionally as Cartomancy, has been practiced for centuries.

In our day and generation divination by cards is chiefly employed for amusement and pastime, for the entertainment of one's self or one's company, or at church fairs, charity bazars, and the like; but in the days of the ancients it was practiced by prophets and sibyls as a serious business, and so accepted by all, from king to peasant.

Certainly there were some remarkable coincidences, to call them by no other name, in the fulfillment of many cartomantic divinations, of which history maintains a record. To cite but one:

THE STORY OF JOSEPHINE, EMPRESS OF THE FRENCH.

Josephine Tascher de la Pagerie, while in her native land of Martinique, had been approached by an aged negress, who astonished her through declaring to her: "You will ascend upon the loftiest throne in the world."

Always treasuring the memory of this prediction, Josephine, when the widow of Gen. Beauharnais, during the bitter days of the Reign of Terror, was induced to consult a distinguished seeress of the Faubourg St. Germain, who relied upon cartomancy as a means for elucidating the mysteries of the past, present, and future. Although her visitor was disguised as a waiting woman, the seeress, through a simple resort to her pack of cards, read most correctly the entire past existence of her consultant. Then, by the same means, she laid bare the gloomy picture of Josephine's present situation; how the prison doors of the Luxembourg stood ready to receive her; how the guillotine thirsted for her life's blood; how, nevertheless, she would be saved from all these impending dangers through intercession of a young soldier, to her at the time personally a stranger. Subsequently, by a fresh appeal to her cards, the seeress threw aside the veil obscuring Josephine's future destiny, predicting her marriage, the onward march of her husband towards fame and power, until finally, after a studious observation of the cards, the cartomancian

Maria D'Andrea's Simple Spells With Playing Cards

announced to her skeptical consultant that on a given day, within the cathedral church of Notre Dame, the unknown man she was destined to marry would place upon her head an imperial diadem, and furthermore that she would be hailed, in the presence of the highest ecclesiastical potentate on earth, as "Empress of the French," and as such would be respected until her death.

The remarkably rapid and literal fulfillment of the predictions made by a professional seeress to an unknown lady, to whom she promised the most exalted of mortal positions, not only astonished the crowd of courtiers, wonder-stricken at realization of this indisputable and well-authenticated augury of miraculous events; but elicited the attention of men of intellect and of science, hundreds of whom visited the remarkable prophetess, and in every instance testified to the accuracy of her predictions, although at a loss to comprehend the source from whence she attained apparently super-human knowledge. It appeared wonderful to these men of science that the mere combination of a series of cards, which they had been accustomed to look upon as a mere species of diversion, could be employed as well to read the past as to penetrate the mysteries of the future; still they were compelled, in an elaborate report made to the Emperor, whose comprehensive mind yearned after explanation of all secrets, mental as well as physical, to state that, while unable to account for the cause for this prophetic knowledge, there could be no rational doubt of its existence.

RESEARCHING GYPSY LORE.

This present treatise on the subject of divination by cards is a gathering together in handy form of the best authenticated methods of its ancient practice as handed down from the Romany gypsies and the seeresses that antedate them. As different nations and different times had their varying interpretations of the values of the cards and separate and distinct methods of laying the cards for readings, as well as fundamental differences in their interpretations of the many possible combinations of the various cards, we have decided to lay before you in this work a complete symposium of each, that the reader and student of the art may see before him all the approved methods of the past and choose intelligently that which best pleases or suits his convenience.

All the old and many of the recent authors that have been consulted in the preparation of this book have been found to insist that divination through playing-cards is to be relied upon as a truthful exposition of the past and future and a veritable portent of the future. They desire to be taken seriously. The present editor has no desire to detract from this position if it be a fact, nor does he know that it is not a fact. His part in this work is that of editor, and there ends. Here he presents you with the results of centuries of effort on the part of those who profess to believe sincerely in what they practice and teach, and leaves the reader to place

Maria D'Andrea's Simple Spells With Playing Cards

as much or as little credence in the truthfulness of their divinations as he chooses.

Certainly there is a wonderful fascination in the mastering of Cartomancy, in the being able to tell fortunes by the chance falling of the cards into this or that position, and in knowing what each card and grouping is believed to signify in their relations to the person consulting.

HOW TO ACQUIRE THE ART.

The would-be adept is advised to study in detail every word in this book, as he would any other lesson he desired to master. Learn the various methods of dealing and of reading the layout; consult the several interpretations of the meanings and learn to apply them, first in reading your own fortune and later that of friends,—this only after you have memorized many of the meanings and acquired a degree of fluency in elaborating the "talk" or "patter" that goes with a successful "reading."

No prophet or seer ever professed that divination by cards is a natural gift. It is universally recognized as being solely the result of study and practice, and can be mastered by anyone who has this book and gives the subject a little thought and sufficient experimental, practical test to acquire proficiency.

CARDS TO BE USED IN TELLING FORTUNES.

While any ordinary pack of playing cards sold in the usual stores can be used, it is best to secure, if possible, a pack whose face cards have only a single head, inasmuch as when, in dealing, cards come out reversed they bear a different signification in some cases, than when upright. When, however, the usual double-headed cards are used it is only necessary to make a distinctive mark on the top end of the faces of certain ones to secure the same result as though the special fortune-telling pack were employed. This mark may be a simple dot or cross with pencil or pen, and should be made at one end of the card only, which will then become the top of the card in all cases, and cards coming out in the deal with this mark at their tops will be considered as upright, and with the marked end down, as reversed. The only cards that need to be thus distinguished are: The face cards of each suit; the ace, eight, nine and ten of diamonds. (The spot cards below the seven in any suit are, in most cases, not used. Where they are employed, their reversal has no significance.) The top of the seven of diamonds, and the other suits, is considered to be the end that has the extra central pip. Spot cards of the three suits other than diamonds usually require no mark to determine their top or bottom. The "handles" of all spades and clubs, and the sharp points of all hearts, point downward when those cards are upright; hence when they point upward the cards are considered as reversed. If, however, any other cards than those here mentioned are so printed as to make it difficult to distinguish the top from the

Maria D'Andrea's Simple Spells With Playing Cards

base, you should mark them at the top.

THE ONE SPECIAL CARD—THE CONSULTANT.

In some of the methods of fortune-telling by cards it is essential to have a special card as the representative of the party seeking the response of the oracle. This is commonly called the "Consultant." If there is a joker in your pack, or an extra blank card, as is the case in many packs, use one of them as the Consultant, marking this card to show which is its top, as its reversal has its own signification. If there is neither joker nor blank card, use the discarded deuce of either suit in the pack, with a mark at its top end.

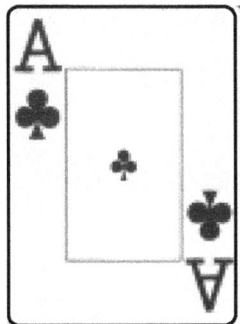  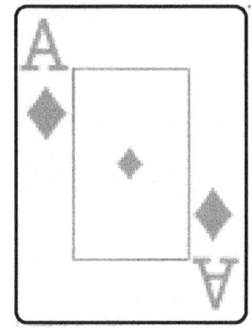 

THE ANCIENT ORACLE

Various meanings have been ascribed to the individual cards in different countries and times, several lists of which, and they the known standards of the art, are given throughout this book. The first list of interpretations that we present is from a very ancient work, first published in 1600 or a little later. This, it will be noticed, defines the entire fifty-two cards of the pack and has no separate signification for any card being upright or reversed; in either position the cards' meanings are the same.

Suit values are as follows: Clubs lead and mostly portend happiness and good business arrangements, and no matter how numerous or how accompanied by cards of other suits are seldom considered as bearers of other than the very best augury. Next comes hearts, which are usually taken to signify love-making, invitations, and good friends; diamonds, money; and spades, annoyances, sickness or worry, sometimes loss of money.

Clubs.

Ace—Great wealth, much prosperity, and tranquillity of mind.

King—A man who is humane, upright and affectionate; faithful in all his undertakings. He will[Pg 13] be happy himself, and make every one around him so.

Queen—A tender, mild and rather susceptible woman, who will be very

Maria D'Andrea's Simple Spells With Playing Cards

attractive to the opposite sex.

Jack—An open, sincere and good friend, who will exert himself warmly in your welfare.

Ten—Speedy wealth.

Nine—Obstinacy and disagreeables connected therewith.

Eight—A covetous person, extremely fond of money; that he will obtain it but not make a proper use of it.

Seven—The most brilliant fortune and the most exquisite bliss this world can afford, but beware of the opposite sex, from these alone can misfortune be experienced.

Six—A lucrative partnership.

Five—Marriage to a person who will improve your circumstances.

Four—Inconstancy and change.

Trey—Three wealthy marriages.

Deuce—Opposition or disappointment.

Diamonds.

Ace—A letter.

King—A man of fiery temper, continued anger, seeking revenge, and obstinate in his resolutions.

Queen—A coquette, and fond of company.

Jack—However nearly related, will look more to[Pg 14] his own interest than yours, will be tenacious in his own opinions, and fly off if contradicted.

Ten—A country husband (or wife), with wealth, and many children; also a purse of gold.

Nine—A surprise about money.

Eight—Unhappy marriage late in life.

Seven—Waste of goods, and losses.

Six—An early marriage and widowhood, but a second marriage would probably be worse.

Five—Success in enterprises; if married, good children.

Four—Vexation and annoyance.

Maria D'Andrea's Simple Spells With Playing Cards

Trey—Quarrels, lawsuits, and domestic disagreements, your partner for life will be a vixen, bad tempered, and make you unhappy.

Deuce—Your heart will be engaged in love at an early period, but you will meet with great opposition.

Hearts.

Ace—Feasting and pleasure, and is also the house. If attended with spades it is quarreling; if by hearts, friendship and affection; if by diamonds, you will hear of an absent friend; if by clubs, merry-making and rejoicing.

King—A man of good natured disposition, hot and hasty, rash in his undertakings, and very amorous.

Queen—A woman of fair complexion, faithful and affectionate.

Jack—A person of no particular sex, but always the dearest friend or nearest relation of the consulting party. It is said that you must pay great attention to the cards that stand next to the jack, as from them alone you are supposed to judge whether the person it represents will be favorable to your inclinations or not.

Ten—A good heart, it is supposed to correct the bad tidings of the cards that stand next it; if its neighboring cards are of good report, it is supposed to confirm their value.

Nine—Wealth, grandeur, and high esteem; if cards that are unfavorable stand near it, disappointments and the reverse. If favorable cards follow these last at a small distance, you will retrieve your losses, whether of peace or goods.

Eight—Drinking and feasting.

Seven—A fickle and unfaithful person.

Six—A generous, open and credulous disposition, easily imposed on, but the friend of the distressed.

Five—A wavering and unsettled disposition.

Four—The person will not be married till quite late in life, which will proceed from too great a delicacy in making a choice.

Trey—Your own imprudence will greatly contribute to your experiencing much ill will from others.

Deuce—Extraordinary good future and success; though if unfavorable cards attend this will be a long time delayed.

Maria D'Andrea's Simple Spells With Playing Cards

Spades.

Ace—Has to do with love affairs generally. Death when the card is upside down.

King—A man ambitious and successful at court, or with a great man who will befriend him, but let him beware of a reverse.

Queen—A woman who will be corrupted by the rich of both sexes. Also a widow.

Jack—A person, who, although he has your interest at heart, will be too indolent to pursue it.

Ten—Is supposed to be a card of bad import, and in a great measure to counteract the good effects of the cards near it.

Nine—Is professed to be the worst card of the pack; dangerous sickness, total loss of fortune and calamities; also endless discussion in your family.

Eight—Opposition from your friends. If this card comes out close to you, leave your plan and follow another.

Seven—Loss of a valuable friend, whose death will plunge you in very great distress.

Six—Very little interpretation of your success.

Five—Good luck in the choice of your companion for life, who will be fond of you. Bad temper and interference.

Four—Sickness.

Trey—Good fortune in marriage, an inconstant partner, and that you will be made unhappy thereby.

Deuce—A death or disagreeable removal.

METHOD A.

Using 52 Cards and the Foregoing Interpretations.

Take a pack of fifty-two cards and shuffle them three times well over, and making the significator whichever queen you please (if a lady performs the operation for herself; or king, if a gentleman), then proceed to lay them on the table, nine in a row, and wherever the operator finds himself placed, count nine cards every way, not forgetting the said significator, then it will be seen what card the significator comes in company with, and read from that.

When several diamonds come together, the interpretation is that some

Maria D'Andrea's Simple Spells With Playing Cards

money will soon be received; several hearts, love; several clubs, drink and noisy troublesome company; several spades, trouble and vexation.

If two red tens come next to the significator marriage or prosperity, the ace of hearts is the house, the ace of clubs a letter, the ace of spades death, spite, or quarreling (for this is supposed to be the worst card in the pack), the ten of diamonds a journey, the three of hearts a salute, the three of spades tears, the ten of spades sickness, the nine of spades sad disappointment or trouble, to the nine of clubs is ascribed a jovial entertainment or reveling, the nine of hearts feasting, the ten of clubs traveling by water, the ten of hearts some place of amusement, the five of hearts a present, the five of clubs a bundle, the six of spades a child, the seven of spades a removal, the three of clubs fighting, the eight of clubs confusion, the eight of spades a roadway, the four of clubs a strange bed, the nine of diamonds business, the five of spades a surprise, the two red eights new clothes, the three of diamonds speaking with a friend, the four of spades a sick bed, the seven of clubs a prison, the two of spades a false friend, the four of hearts the marriage bed.

If a married lady doth lay the cards, she must then make her husband the king of the same suit she is queen of; but if a single lady, she must make her lover what king she may think proper. The jacks of the same suits are supposed to be men's thoughts, so that they may know what they are thinking of, counting nine cards from where they are placed, and it is said if any lady should wish to know whether she shall obtain her desires in any particular subject, matter, or thing whatsoever, let her shuffle the cards well, most seriously and earnestly wishing all the time for one thing; she must then cut them once, particularly observing at the same time what card that is which she cuts, then shuffle them and deal them out in three parcels, and if that said particular card which she has cut doth come next herself, or next the ace of hearts, it is taken that she will have her wish, but if the nine of spades is next to her she judges the contrary, as that is supposed to be a disappointment; however, she may try it three times, taking the major number of testimonies as a ground whereon to place her judgment. This method of using the cards is both innocent and will afford amusement.

MODERN USE OF 52 CARDS

Here we present the more modern adaptation of the entire pack of 52 cards to the fortune-teller's use. As the meanings differ materially from the ancient list just given, another complete list and several combinations are presented.

In the modern usage, Diamonds take precedence and are considered to mean money, riches and success.

Hearts next, love affairs, friendship, amusement and pleasure.

Maria D'Andrea's Simple Spells With Playing Cards

Clubs, business matters, whether investments, appointments or settlements.

Spades, losses or grief, trouble and anxiety, sometimes sickness and death.

The various combinations are supposed to either accelerate or mitigate the several meanings.

For instance—the ace of diamonds coming with the ace of spades, a railway journey—the nine of spades, usually taken to be a bad card, but coming with diamonds, speedy good luck, etc.

Diamonds.

Ace—An offer or a ring.

King—A fair man, a military man, or a diplomatist.

Queen—A fair woman, fond of pleasure and amusement.

Jack—The thoughts of either king or queen.

Ten—A legacy or property.

Nine—A good surprise about money.

Eight—Meetings about money matters.

Seven—A check or paper money; sometimes scandal.

Six—An offer of some kind, generally to do with money matters.

Five (supposed to be the best card in the pack)—Health, wealth and happiness.

Four—A short journey.

Three—Time, within three to four weeks.

Two—A secret or something unexpected.

Hearts.

Ace—The house.

King—A rather fair man in society; sometimes a sailor.

Queen—A fair woman in society, but kind and good natured.

Jack—Thoughts of either king or queen.

Ten—An entertainment or festivity.

Nine—Great happiness and the wish card.

Eight—Love making or friendship.

Maria D'Andrea's Simple Spells With Playing Cards

Seven—A puzzle or indecision, doubt.

Six—Love affairs, sometimes an offer.

Five—Marriage, sometimes a new admirer.

Four—A small invitation, such as a dinner or evening party.

Three—Time, within a week.

Two—Kisses or trifling present.

Clubs.

Ace—A letter.

King—A clever dark man, often a professional man, or in business.

Queen—A clever, amusing woman, sometimes a little satirical.

Jack—Thoughts of king or queen.

Ten—A new appointment, investment or settlement.

Nine—Relates to documents, papers, often a will.

Eight—A journey by road or vehicle.

Seven—A warning or unprofitable business.

Six—A very poor business offer or else money borrowed.

Five—News, either from the country or some one coming therefrom.

Four—A journey by land on business.

Three—Time, three to four months.

Two—A good friend, in some cases a slight disappointment.

Spades.

Ace—Spite, death, or worry; sometimes a large town.

King—A lawyer, widower or old man; a very dark man.

Queen—A very dark woman, a widow; a spiteful, malicious woman.

Jack—Thoughts of king or queen.

Ten—At night-time, imprisonment.

Nine (supposed to be a very bad card)—Grief, suffering, malice, and, with other black cards, death.

Eight—Across water, sometimes treachery.

Maria D'Andrea's Simple Spells With Playing Cards

Seven—Poverty, anxiety and annoyance.

Six—Delay, or a bad character.

Five—Temper, anger and quarrels.

Four—Sickness, sometimes a journey caused through sickness.

Three—By the water, or a very short journey across water.

Two—Tears and vexation, sometimes a removal.

The following is a *résumé* of most of the cards and some curious combinations:

Four Aces—Honors, dignities, rise in society, or money, friendship with the great; but if all four are reversed, the contrary—debt, bankruptcy, ruin and even disgrace, therefore it is to be noticed particularly how they lie before reading the cards.

Four Kings—Great good luck, unexpected advancement, good and unlooked-for fortune.

Four Queens—Society, pleasure, amusements.

Four Jacks—Thoughts of either king or queen of each suit, friendly gathering.

Four Tens—Great gain, legacies, happiness.

Four Nines—Unexpected and sudden news; if two blacks together, not pleasant; if two reds, excellent.

Four Eights—New appointments, sometimes new associations; two black eights together, mourning; two reds, wedding garments.

Four Sevens—Intrigues, scandal, opposition and variance.

Four Sixes—A great surprise or change; two black ones together, vexations; two red ones, good.

Four Fives—A long and beneficial voyage, money, happiness and health; if two blacks are near, vexation first.

Four Fours—A birth; two blacks together, a male; two reds, a female.

Four Threes—Period of time from six to twelve months; sometimes gain or money returned.

Four Twos—Visitors; two blacks together, disagreeable; two reds, pleasant, and sometimes love-making.

Maria D'Andrea's Simple Spells With Playing Cards

Three Aces—Great good luck.

Three Kings—A new friend or acquaintance who will advance you in life.

Three Queens—Quarrels, disputes, backbiting.

Three Jacks—A lawsuit or treachery.

Three Tens—A rise in social life, but not necessarily happiness with it.

Three Nines—A good removal, unless accompanied by very bad cards.

Three Eights—Love dreams, and longing for the unattainable, but often wishes or desires postponed; in some cases fresh engagements, but a little worry in obtaining them.

Three Sevens—Losses of friendship or property; reversed, you will never recover your goods.

Three Sixes—A very large and brilliant entertainment; if the two black ones come together, disgrace or scandal.

Three Fives—A delightful and happy meeting with absent friends.

Three Fours—Strangers or visitors coming to the house from a journey.

Three Threes—Slight annoyances or vexation caused by malicious tongues.

Three Twos—A good and staunch friend, but one who will grieve you by a queer temper.

Two Aces—Strange news quick and speedy, often good luck; two blacks, a telegram; two reds, a pleasant invitation.

Two Kings—A partnership or friendship.

Two Queens—A good female friend.

Two Jacks—Unpleasantness, sometimes only thoughts of people.

Two Tens—Change of residence or profession.

Two Nines—A good removal, sometimes business projects or documents, in many cases relating to a will.

Two Eights—An extraordinary occurrence.

Two Sevens—Sometimes sudden and unexpected; two blacks, great treachery, especially if reversed.

Two Sixes—A good friend; two blacks, a nasty, deceitful person, or a great danger, possibly an accident.

Maria D'Andrea's Simple Spells With Playing Cards

Two Black Fives—Danger from falls, or possibly by water.

Two Red Fives—Joyful and unexpected news.

Two Black Fours—Separation or unfriendly meetings.

Two Red Fours—Good appointments, or good luck.

Two Red Threes—Pleasant and profitable visitors and friends.

Two Black Threes—Disappointment and tears.

Two Black Twos—A departure.

Two Red Twos—An arrival.

The Ace, Nine, Ten and Seven of Spades—Divorce.

Seven and Nine of Spades—Separation.

Eight of Spades and Seven of Clubs—Prison, or confinement.

Six and Four of Spades—Sickness and danger.

Eight and Five of Spades—Malignity, caused by jealousy.

Six and Seven of Spades—Treachery, scandal, vexation.

Seven and Two of Spades—Tears caused by unfounded reports—often a false friend.

Nine and Six of Spades—A bitter and implacable enemy; if good cards follow, you will overcome, but if bad ones, he or she will triumph.

Three and Two of Spades—A short and not agreeable journey.

Seven of Hearts and Three of Spades—A journey and a strange adventure thereon.

Seven, Six and Five of Spades—Thieves, or danger of robbery.

Queen and Jack of Spades—Widowhood.

Nine and Ten of Spades—Danger by fire.

Six and Seven of Spades reversed—A fall or injury.

Eight and Ten of Spades—News at night, but not very pleasant.

Ten, Eight and Five of Spades—Broken engagement, or unfulfilled promise.

Six and Eight of Spades—Delay, postponement.

Nine, Seven, Six and Five of Spades—Bankruptcy.

Maria D'Andrea's Simple Spells With Playing Cards

Ace of Diamonds and Ten of Hearts—A marriage engagement.

Ace of Diamonds and Nine of Hearts—Hopes fulfilled.

Ten of Hearts and Four of Hearts—Marriage.

Three Tens and Five of Hearts—Happy love returned.

Eight of Hearts and Seven of Hearts—Doubt and indecision about an offer.

Seven of Hearts reversed—A nice and good present.

Three of Diamonds and Three of Hearts—In nine days.

Nine of Hearts and Nine of Diamonds—A delightful surprise about money.

Nine of Hearts and Nine of Clubs—Something to do about a will, in which the consultor is generally successful.

Eight of Hearts and Nine of Hearts—Great good luck through love.

Ace, Nine, Seven and Four of Spades—Death.

METHOD B.

A pack of fifty-two cards is taken, shuffled, and cut in three; the first ten are taken out, then three are missed; another nine are taken out, then two are missed; another seven out, five missed; seven out, three missed; three out, one missed; and the last of the pack is taken. They are now laid out in rows of eight each, eight having been counted every way, beginning from the significator. When all are finished, the two extremities are taken, paired and read; they are then gathered together, shuffled, and cut in four parcels; the first one of each parcel is taken off and put on one side. The packet that comes first is the one that should be read.

METHOD C.

What is Supposed to Happen Within a Month to Two Months.

A pack of fifty-two cards is taken, shuffled and cut in three, each meaning being read as it turns up. The cards are then turned up one by one till a spade is found, which is not withdrawn, but the following card, which lay face uppermost on the table. If three spades are found in succession the first is missed, but the two next are taken out, as well as the following card, whether diamonds, clubs or hearts; this is continued to the end of the pack, then re-commenced without shuffling or cutting. Should the final card have been a spade, on beginning the pack afresh the first card should be taken out. The same operation is gone through twice more, in all three times. This having been done, they are laid in the form of a horseshoe in front of the dealer in the order in which they came, being careful to note that the significator is amongst them. Should it not appear naturally, it must be taken out

Maria D'Andrea's Simple Spells With Playing Cards

and placed at the end. Seven are now counted from the one that represents the person consulting the oracle. When they have been read, and the relative meanings ascribed to them explained, one is taken from each end and paired, their various significations being interpreted as they turn up. These prognostications are supposed to come to pass within two months. A shorter way can be done by taking out thirty-two selected cards, viz:—ace, king, queen, jack, ten, nine, eight and seven of each suit; they are read in precisely the same way. This is taken to allow a shorter period to elapse, from ten days to a fortnight, but the former is supposed to be the better method.

METHOD D.

A pack of fifty-two cards is taken, and after being well shuffled they are turned up one by one, counting one, two, three, four, five, six, seven, eight, nine, ten, jack, queen, king (here the ace counts as one). If any card should fall on the number counted—thus, supposing a five comes when five is counted, or a king when that card turns up, it must be taken out and placed on the table, face uppermost, before the dealer. After counting to a king the counting is re-commenced at one. Should two cards follow, such as three and four, eight and nine, etc., these must be abstracted, also three of a kind, such as three tens, three kings, etc., they must also be taken out; but if three of the same suit they may be passed by. When the pack has been carefully gone through, shuffled and cut, the process is gone through twice more, in all three times. They are now all laid out in rows of four and read. When this is done they are gathered together and laid two by two, thus:—

NORTH.

WEST.

EAST.

SOUTH.

One, two, three, four, five, six, seven, eight, nine, ten, eleven, twelve, thirteen, fourteen, fifteen, sixteen, and so on till the pack is exhausted. Those at the top are the North, those at the bottom are the South, those at the right hand the East, those at the left hand the West. The North is to be read first, as that is supposed to happen first; the South next, the East next, and the West last.

METHOD E.

The pack of fifty-two cards is taken, shuffled, and cut in three, the meanings of the cut being read first. Then the significator is taken out. The cards are spread on the table, face downwards before the dealer, and seven are drawn out at ran-

Maria D'Andrea's Simple Spells With Playing Cards

dom. The topmost card of the seven is taken off and put on one side. The cards are again shuffled and cut in three, the cut again read as before; they are laid on the table, seven cards being taken off, the topmost being withdrawn. This is to be repeated the third time, still taking off the topmost card. The cards are again shuffled and cut, this time nine each time being drawn out and the topmost two removed. This maneuver has to be repeated three times, each time taking two of the topmost cards. In the first deal, where the first seven cards were removed, there will be eighteen cards; the second time there will be twenty-one remaining after having removed the two of each cut, thus:—The thirty-nine cards are spread out in five rows of seven, and four remaining underneath. The significator is now put in the center, and counting every way from it, these cards are taken to signify the past and present. The nine cards that have been taken from each sevens and nines are to be shuffled and looked at. These are supposed to refer entirely to the future. The three cards that are left out are useless.

METHOD F—THE STAR.

The pack of fifty-two cards is taken, shuffled, and cut in three, the cut being explained as it is shown. The card representing the significator should be taken out and put in the middle. Three cards are now placed above the head, three at the feet, three to the left, and three to the right, three at the four corners, and three across the significator. They are interpreted as follows:—First, above the head, then at the feet, then to the right hand, and next to the left; each corner to be taken top and bottom opposite. When these are all explained (those across the significator last), they are then paired, beginning with the topmost cards and the bottom cards, from end to end.

METHOD G—A SHORTER STAR.

This is a much shorter way, and instead of placing the cards as they come, they must be first well shuffled by the person consulting, then laid face downwards on the table and nine cards withdrawn (the significator must be in the center). In this method the cards are placed round the card representing the consultor in the order in which they come, the first card drawn being put at the head of the significator, and the others in rotation. The nine cards are first explained as they lie, eight round and one over the significator. Then the consultor is desired to again draw nine, and these are put over the first nine; this is to be repeated a third time, combining all the cards as they lay one over the other, three deep, every way.

METHOD H.

The whole pack is taken, shuffled well, but not cut, every fifth card is picked out and laid by, the pack is gone through and every seventh card picked out,

Maria D'Andrea's Simple Spells With Playing Cards

every third card must be taken, each fifth, seventh and third cards to be laid aside in separate packets; then each packet is carefully examined, whether the significator is amongst those withdrawn. If not, he or she must be abstracted and placed at the extreme end. Now the third pack is laid out in a row, the second next, and the first last, and all that is hidden is said to be shown you, counting three, seven and five from each row, beginning with the significator. Now two are taken from end to end and read till twelve are obtained; they are put on one side; then the rest are gone on with from end to end until all are exhausted. Then they are all taken up, including the twelve that were put aside, shuffled, the two first and last are taken off. These three form "the surprise"; then parcels of four are dealt, beginning with the first; they are all read in rotation and the small "surprise" last.

METHOD I.

The pack of fifty-two cards is taken, shuffled, cut in three, and the meanings ascribed to the cut are explained. Then they are laid in rows of five till the whole pack is exhausted, except the two last, which are useless. The first row is to represent "the person for whom you are acting"; the second, "the house"; the third, "your wish"; the fourth, "the surprise," and the fifth, "what is supposed to come true." The first ten are now read *lengthwise*, the others in the same manner till the fifth row has been explained; then they are taken from end to end, each pair being interpreted as arrived at. In this case there is no significator, as the first row is supposed to stand for what will happen immediately to the consultant. They are all gathered together, shuffled and cut, and laid in packets of three. The consultor is desired to choose one of the three parcels, and that is laid out first and explained; then follow each of the other two, which must be also read in the same manner.

METHOD J.

The pack of fifty-two cards is taken, shuffled and cut by the person consulting. They are cut in three and the meanings interpreted. Then they are laid out in rows of sevens, leaving the three last, which are not to be used. Then nine are counted every way, from the significator backwards and forwards, from left to right, and from right to left, up and down, always returning to the significator, then crossways from end to end. Then they are paired from corner to corner, each card being explained as it is arrived at, noticing if there should be any pairs, triplets, etc., amongst them. Then they are gathered up and shuffled well, then they are dealt in two packets, the consultant being desired to choose one. The one taken is supposed to represent the past and present, the other the future. They are laid out and read pretty much as before.

METHOD K.

Maria D'Andrea's Simple Spells With Playing Cards

A pack of fifty-two cards is taken, shuffled and cut, and divided thus:—Every seven, nine and five are to be removed and put on one side. The six of clubs, the eight and ten of diamonds are to be withdrawn and put in a place by themselves. Then the rest are shuffled and five cards laid out face upwards till the pack is exhausted. It will now be found there are seven rows of five cards each, and two remaining; these two are placed with the nines, sevens and fives, to be used later. These cards are read, counting seven every way from the significator, then gathered together, shuffled and cut, the first group (seven in number) being first of all withdrawn, which must be added to the nines, sevens and fives already withdrawn. There will now be four groups of seven cards each.

The first must be read, the second put aside, the third explained, and the fourth laid by. The second and fourth are left out entirely and not used. The nines, sevens and fives and the first group you have withdrawn are shuffled, cut in two packets, and laid out on the table before the dealer. If two red nines appear close together, it is taken to show honor, dignity and joy; if two red sevens and two red fives side by side, great and unexpected good luck, a legacy or money that you don't anticipate; if two red fives and the nine of hearts are near each other, a marriage of affection; if with the seven of diamonds, a moneyed marriage, but of love; if two red fives and two black sevens, a marriage for money which will turn out unhappily; if two red sevens and two red fives, and the nine of hearts appear, it is supposed to be the greatest and happiest prognostic you can have, whether married or single—luck, pleasure, money; if two black sevens and two black fives appear, it is considered very evil, and if accompanied by the nine of spades, unhappiness in marriage, divorce, scandal and sometimes violence caused through drink; if the eight of spades should be amongst those withdrawn and turn up with the aforesaid cards, violent death by murder or accident. It is taken to be the worst combination in the pack.

These cards (viz: the nines, sevens and fives, and those which have been withdrawn from the group of fives) are laid in rows of sevens, counting seven every way from the significator; then the extreme ends are taken and paired, being read as they turn up. Next the whole is shuffled, including the six of clubs and the eight and ten of diamonds. These three cards are the index. Wherever they appear they are supposed to show good luck, happiness and prosperity; if they should happen between exceptionally bad cards, the luck is over, or marred through malignity; but as a rule they are taken to import great joy.

The evil combination is thus: If the six of clubs is surrounded with spades, or the eight or ten of diamonds are *between* two black fives and the two black sevens are near, then the best laid scheme will come to nought; but if they are surrounded by the nine of hearts and nine of diamonds, then it is a very good omen. The eight and ten of diamonds are supposed to be extremely good if there

Maria D'Andrea's Simple Spells With Playing Cards

are three or four nines to follow them, for then the nine of spades loses its evil significance, and should the seven of diamonds and seven of hearts follow, a good marriage and happiness; or, if the person is married, new prosperity or riches for the husband or sometimes the birth of an heir.

METHOD L.

The pack of fifty-two cards is taken, shuffled and cut, and divided into two equal heaps. One of these is chosen by the consultant. Having decided this, the other heap is left alone; it is not to be used. The person consulting is now desired to shuffle the twenty-six cards remaining, cutting in three, the meanings being read as they turn up. They are now dealt in three packs, which are laid out in rows of eight, the last card to be left out, as that forms "the surprise." Four cards are now counted from the significator, which, should it not be in the pack chosen, must be abstracted and put at the end. When these have been fully explained, the same maneuver is repeated twice, in all three times, one card being always taken out for "the surprise." "The surprise" is turned up when those cards before the dealer have been examined and explained. Then they are all gathered together, and, after being shuffled and cut, they are turned up by fours. If a sequence should come up, such as six and seven, or six, seven and eight of any suit, they are taken out. If four of a suit, the lowest is taken out. This is only to be done once. These are now laid out in a row before the dealer and read from left to right, always taking note that the significator is amongst them, and counting four as above described. Then the two cards are taken from each extremity and each couple explained till all are exhausted.

METHOD M.

A pack of fifty-two cards is taken, shuffled well and cut. Then it is divided into three equal parcels of seventeen cards each, and one over for "the surprise," which is to be laid aside. The first three cards of each packet is taken, and each three is put apart. That will leave fourteen in each group. The first and third packets of fourteen are taken up, the middle one being put aside. These are now laid out in four rows of seven, being sure that the significator is amongst them; or else the card which is supposed to represent the thoughts of the person consulting you, viz: the jack, may be counted from. Six are now counted, beginning from the next card to the significator; and after every sixth card, that card is not counted as one, but the following one. When these have been explained, which must be done till the significator is returned to, they are paired from end to end, and read as arrived at; then they are gathered together, shuffled and cut, and divided again into two groups of fourteen. These are not laid out again, but two being merely extracted from each of these, not forgetting the middle one, and adding them to the three packets of three placed on one side. The middle one is now taken up,

Maria D'Andrea's Simple Spells With Playing Cards

shuffled well, and four cards taken from it, two from the top and two from the bottom, and added to the one put aside to form "the surprise." There are now four packs of five cards each:—One for the "consultant" and one for the "house," one for "what is sure to come true," and one for "the surprise." These are laid out in front of the dealer and read from left to right in rotation.

THE PREFERRED ORACLE—WITH 32 CARDS

We now come to the most important and approved method of telling fortunes by cards, the method preferred and practiced in nearly all countries. This widely accepted method requires but 32 cards of the 52 found in the pack, consisting of eight cards of each suit, as follows: Ace, king, queen, jack, ten, nine, eight and seven only. To these may be added, in some cases, the Consultant card, concerning which we have spoken earlier in this work.

To enable this oracle to be read with an intelligent and proper understanding it is important that one be fully informed as to all the possible values or interpretations of the cards, singly and in combination. Hence we shall devote a number of pages to these definitions in very complete form before proceeding to elucidate for you the various methods of dealing, laying and reading the cards. We give first the simple and primary meanings, followed in detail by their secondary or synonymical meanings, the whole constituting a valuable work of reference for all who practice the art, enabling them to give a full, fair and wise reading of every possible "fall" of the cards. The primary meanings, while sufficient for the amateur, will soon be seen by the student to be lacking in that completeness and flexibility demanded by the adept. Their natural amplification into their secondary and more extended definitions gives the interpreter the fullest scope to exercise his powers of reading any possible layout of the cards intelligently, and with satisfaction both to himself and to the person consulting the oracle.

DICTIONARY OF PRIMARY DEFINITIONS

Used in Interpreting the 32-Card Method of Telling Fortunes.

Diamonds.

KING

Upright—Marriage. A military man. A man of fidelity. A dignitary of the state. A very fair person. A man of tact and cunning.

Reversed—A country gentleman. A difficulty concerning marriage or business. Threatened danger, caused through the machination of a man in position or office.

Maria D'Andrea's Simple Spells With Playing Cards

QUEEN

Upright—A blonde female. A lady resident in the country. A woman given to gossiping and scandal.

Reversed—A country gentlewoman. A malignant female, who seeks to foment disadvantage to the consultant, and who is to be greatly feared.

JACK

Upright—A country man. A young man of light complexion, of a lower grade in society. A messenger. Postman. A tale-bearing servant, or unfaithful friend.

Reversed—A servant. An intermeddler, who will be the cause of mischief. A messenger bearing ill-news.

ACE

Upright—The ace of diamonds, whether upright or reversed, signifies a letter, a petition, a note, a paper, a document.

Reversed—The ace of diamonds, reversed or upright, designates a letter to be shortly received, a petition, a note, a paper, or a document.

TEN

Upright—The ten of diamonds, either upright or reversed, represents coin, gold, water, the sea, a foreign city, and change of locality.

Reversed—The ten of diamonds, whether reversed or upright, designates bullion, coin, gold, water, the ocean, a foreign city, a journey and change in locality.

NINE

Upright—Enterprise. Separation. Advantage.

Reversed—Delay. Annoyance. Poverty. A family feud, or a quarrel among intimate friends.

EIGHT

Upright—The country. Riches. Love-making overtures.

Reversed—Sorrow. Motion. Wealth. Satire. Mockery, and foolish scandal.

SEVEN

Upright—Present intentions. Good news.

Reversed—Birth. Contrariness. Vexation. In a great measure.

Maria D'Andrea's Simple Spells With Playing Cards

Hearts.

KING

Upright—A blonde man. A lawyer. A man of repute, and remarkable for superior qualities. A person of generosity.

Reversed—A very fair man. A tutor. A man in anger. Great disappointment.

QUEEN

Upright—A blonde female. A faithful friend. A mild, amiable lady.

Reversed—A very fair female. Impediment to marriage. Obstacle to success in business and general affairs. A woman crossed in love.

JACK

Upright—A blonde young man. A young soldier or sailor. A traveler. A gay young bachelor, dreaming chiefly of his pleasures.

Reversed—A very fair young man. A dissipated bachelor. A discontented military man. A politician out of office.

ACE

Upright—The house. A repast. Festivity. A love letter. Agreeable intelligence.

Reversed—A friend's visit. Forced or constrained enjoyment.

TEN

Upright—The city. Envious people.

Reversed—An inheritance. A surprise.

NINE

Upright—Victory. Happiness. Triumph. Union. Harmony. Work. Trade. A present.

Reversed—Weariness. Ennui. A passing trouble. Curiosity. Encumbrance.

EIGHT

Upright—The affection of a fair young lady. Success in your hopes. Nourishment. Food. Board.

Reversed—A very fair maiden. Excessive joy. A young woman's indifference to love advances.

Maria D'Andrea's Simple Spells With Playing Cards

SEVEN

Upright—The thoughts. A weapon. A jewel.

Reversed—Desire. A parcel.

Spades.

KING

Upright—A dark complexioned man. A gentleman of some learned profession. A judge. Advocate. Surgeon. Physician. A literary man.

Reversed—A widower. A man in wrath or with a malignant disposition. An envious man. Dishonest lawyer. A quack. An enemy. A general failure in all your anticipations.

QUEEN

Upright—A dark complexioned woman. A widow. A lady of some learned profession.

Reversed—A widow seeking to marry again. A dangerous and malicious woman. A fast female. Difficulty. Derangement as to marriage.

JACK

Upright—A dark complexioned bachelor. An envoy. An ill-bred fellow. A messenger.

Reversed—An inquisitive, impertinent interloper. A man plotting mischief. A spy. Pursuit. Treason in love affairs.

ACE

Upright—Abandonment. A document.

Reversed—Pregnancy. Abandonment. Grief. Distressing intelligence.

TEN

Upright—Tears. Jealousy.

Reversed—Loss. An evening party. Brief affliction. In the evening.

NINE

Upright—A great loss. Tidings of death. Mourning. Failure.

Reversed—Disappointment. Delay. Desertion. Tidings of the death of a near relative.

Maria D'Andrea's Simple Spells With Playing Cards

EIGHT

Upright—Sickness. Want of prudence. Bad news.

Reversed—Ambition. A religious woman. A marriage broken off, or an offer refused.

SEVEN

Upright—Expectation. Hope.

Reversed—Wise advice. Friendship. Indecision. A foolish intrigue.

Clubs.

KING

Upright—A man whose complexion is between light and dark. A frank, liberal man. A friend.

Reversed—A nut-brown complexioned man. A person to meet with a disappointment.

QUEEN

Upright—A brunette female. One fond of conversation. An affectionate, quick tempered woman.

Reversed—A nut-brown complexioned lady. A jealous and malicious female.

JACK

Upright—A slightly dark complexioned bachelor. A lover. A clever and enterprising young man.

Reversed—A flirt and flatterer. A young man in anger or in sickness.

ACE

Upright—A purse of money. Wealth.

Reversed—Nobility. Love. A present.

TEN

Upright—The house. The future. Fortune. Success. Gain. Money.

Reversed—Money. A lover. Sometimes want of success in a trivial matter.

NINE

Upright—Chattels. Goods. Movable article. An indiscretion.

Reversed—A trifling present. Gambling.

Maria D'Andrea's Simple Spells With Playing Cards

EIGHT

Upright—The affections of a brunette maiden. The art of pleasing.

Reversed—A nut-brown maiden. Removal. Separation. A frivolous courtship.

SEVEN

Upright—A small sum of money. A debt unexpectedly paid. A child.

Reversed—A child. Embarrassment.

THE CONSULTANT.

When coming out in an upright position, in the body of the deal designates merely the person consulting the oracle, in a natural state of mind.

When the card comes out in the deal reversed, it denotes the consultant to be in a disturbed state of mind, or annoyed from some cause beyond his or her control. Coming with the *eight of spades reversed*, for example, by its side, it shows that the consultant's mind has been disordered through prospects of ambition or religious excitement. If accompanied by the *eight of hearts*, it demonstrates that he or she is annoyed through being a victim to the tender passion.

DICTIONARY OF SECONDARY DEFINITIONS

And Synonyms, Supplementing the Preceding List. Consult Both.

King of Diamonds—*Upright*. This card, when used as a representative, denotes a very fair man, one with auburn hair, light blue eyes, and florid complexion, who, notwithstanding his hasty temper, will treasure his anger, long awaiting opportunities for revenge, or he is obstinate in his resolutions.

It moreover designates a military officer, and frequently one of fidelity to his country and its honor.

Still, it is most generally employed as the marriage card, for if it does not come out in an oracle wherein matrimony is the wish, the nuptials will be delayed or broken off.

Its synonymical signification would then be:

Alliance; reunion; attachment; vow; oath; intimacy; assemblage; junction; union; chain; peace; accord; harmony; good understanding; reconciliation.

King of Diamonds—*Reversed*. This card signifies a country gentleman, in which capacity its synonyms are:

Country man; rustic; villager; peasant; farm laborer; cultivator; rural; agriculture.

Maria D'Andrea's Simple Spells With Playing Cards

Again, this card reversed, bears a further signification of a good and severe man, when its synonyms would be:

Indulgent severity; indulgence; compliance; condescension; complacency; tolerance; low descension.

When used as the marriage card, and coming out reversed, the king of diamonds signifies primarily difficulties and obstacles imposed in the way of entering upon or consummating the nuptial contract, and through inference vitiation of the married state, when its synonyms are:

Slavery; captivity; servitude; matrimonial ruptures; conjugal infidelity.

Queen of Diamonds—*Upright*. When this card comes out in the oracle upright it bears three primary significations: *a country lady*; *a talkative* or *communicative female*; and a *good, kind-hearted woman*.

As a representative card it designates a very fair female with auburn or blonde hair, brilliantly clear complexion and very blue eyes. A woman of this character will be given to society, and is naturally a coquette.

When the card is taken as a *country lady* its synonyms will be through induction or inference:

Economical housewife; chaste and honest woman; honesty; civility; politeness; sweetness of temper; virtue; honor; chastity; a model wife; excellent mother.

When used to designate a *talkative female*, they will be:

Conversation; discourse; deliberation; dissertation; discussion; conference; intellectual entertainment; prattler; blab; idle talk; flippant conversation; table talk; gossip.

Queen of Diamonds—*Reversed*. When the card comes out reversed in the oracle its ordinary signification is that of a meddlesome woman, who has interfered in the affairs of the consultant for the purpose of doing him or her injury, and the extent of the injury, contemplated or done, can be estimated from the proximity of this card to that of the consultant, or from the import of those cards intervening between the two. This card has two secondary significations as follows:

Want of foresight, whose synonyms are:

Unawares; unexpectedly; on a sudden; napping; astonished; suddenly; fortuitously; unhoped for; surprisingly.

A knavish trick, whose synonyms would be:

Roguishness; knavery; cheat; imposture; deceit; sharpness in rascality; trickery; false pretense; artifice; wile; craftiness.

Maria D'Andrea's Simple Spells With Playing Cards

Jack of Diamonds—*Upright*. The primary signification of this card is a *soldier*, a *postillion*, or a light haired *young man, in or from the country*. In addition to these characteristics this card, whether upright or reversed, assumes another, which is technically called *the good stranger*.

As a *soldier*, its secondary value is expressed in the following synonyms:

Man at arms; swordsman; fencing master; combatant; enemy; duel; war; battle; attack; defense; opposition; resistance; ruin; overthrow; hostility; hatred; wrath; resentment; courage; valor; bravery; satellite; stipendiary.

In the quality of *the good stranger*, its synonyms are:

Strange; unaccustomed; unknown; unheard of; unusual; unwonted; surprising; admirable; marvelous; prodigious; miracle; episode; digression; anonymous.

When employed as a representative of a person, it denotes a light haired, unmarried man, who, although one of your nearest relations, will sacrifice your interests to his own; a person of stubbornness; hot headed and hasty, tenacious of his own opinions and unable to brook contradiction.

Jack of Diamonds—*Reversed*. This card's signification is a public or private servant; and in the latter case, without reference to gender, either a male or female domestic. Its synonyms therefore are in accordance with its acceptation:

Servant; waiter; valet; chambermaid; lady's maid; a subordinate; an inferior; a hireling; condition of one employed; servitude; postman; errand boy; messenger; agent; expressman; newsman; message; announcement; commission; directions; a household; relative to post office and the transmission of messages.

Ace of Diamonds—It is a matter of perfect indifference whether this card assumes its place in the oracle in an upright or reversed position, as its primary signification is in no wise varied, although of a most comprehensive nature, being, expressing generally, a *letter*, a *note*, a *paper*, a *petition*, etc.

It requires, however, a great deal of attention to discriminate between the manifold significations of this all-important card, which is governed in a great measure by the cards coming next to it, otherwise the interpreter may be entirely baffled in comprehending the intent of the oracle.

The general synonyms of the *ace of diamonds* are:

Epistle; writings; the art of writing; grammar; Holy Writ; text; literature; doctrine; erudition; literary labor; book; correspondence; composition; alphabet; elements of all learning; principles; bonds; bills of exchange; notes of hand; evidence of indebtedness.

With the *seven of spades, reversed*, coming next to it, this card denotes the

Maria D'Andrea's Simple Spells With Playing Cards

existence of a law suit, in which case we have synonyms, founded on the following basis:

Deed; covenant; agreement; law paper; writs; warrants; litigation; differences; contestations; disputes; discussions; bickering; contest; strife; discord; contradiction; stratagem; trick; broil; pettifogging; wrangling.

Ten of Diamonds—Like its companion, the *ace*, which with this card form the only two in the pack possessing this peculiar quality, the *ten of diamonds* preserves its value and signification, whether it emerges either upright or reversed. The primary significations of this card are *gold*, *water*, the *sea*, a *foreign city*, *change of locality*.

As the representative of *gold* its synonyms are:

Riches; opulence; magnificence; splendor; éclat; sumptuousness; luxury; abundance; means.

When its signification is assumed relative to *water* and the *sea*, the synonyms assume both a specific and general nature:

Fluid; humid; ablution; dew; rain; deluge; inundation; the ocean; river; torrent; stream; fountain; source; lake; pond; cascade; falls.

When the surrounding cards designate this one to be accepted as representing a foreign city, its synonyms are:

Traveler; traveling; foreign parts; beyond the sea; homeless; wanderer; wandering abroad; trading; commerce; a sailor; ships; refuge; exile.

When accepted to signify a *change in locality*, the synonyms, in addition to preservation of its original meaning of a mere change in domicile, or habitation, are inferentially extended to embrace a wider scope, such as:

Departure; displacement; journey; pilgrimage; peregrination; steps; motion; visits; excursions; incursions; emigration; immigration; transmigration; flight; tour; rotation; circulation; deportation; rout; defeat; overthrow; bewilderment; disconcert; to break one's allegiance; desertion; disinheritance; alienation; alien; a foreigner; houseless.

It will be seen that with the varied significations which can be given to this card, it is one of the most important in the pack.

Nine of Diamonds—*Upright.* When coming forth in its natural position, this card is one of particular good omen, as it foretells great success in business operations and consequent gain. Its primary meaning comprehends the grand mainspring to human exertion, *enterprise*, while at the same time it assures you of the desired result, *advantage* or *gain*. Viewed as such its synonyms are, as to *enter-*

Maria D'Andrea's Simple Spells With Playing Cards

prise in the first instance:

To undertake; to commence; to usurp; to take possession of; audacity; boldness; hardihood; impudence; rashness; speculative; speculation; fearless in trade; in love.

When taken to represent *advantage*, the synonyms are:

Gain; profit; lucre; success; thanks; favor; bene[Pg 56]fit; ascendency; power; empire; authority; government; rule; glory; reputation; happy results; profitable end; victory; cure; fulfillment; termination; satisfaction.

Nine of Diamonds—*Reversed.* We have the other side of the picture, for this card, coming up reversed portends the occurrence of dire mishaps and abject despoliation with its concomitant poverty. In view of this immense difference in the value and signification of this one and the same card in its two positions, too much care cannot be taken to mark the way in which it emerges.

In its modified signification of *delay*, its synonyms are:

Disarranged; sent back; suspension; variation; wavering; slowness; relenting; obstacle; impediment; misfortune; adversity; accidental injuries; miscarriage.

But viewed in its more bitter light as *spoliation* and *poverty*, its synonyms are:

Destitution; violence; ruin; victim of robbery; a fall; ruined honor; bankruptcy; privation; violated chastity; defrauded; swindled; victimized; separation; sold out by the sheriff; cast upon the town; hopeless.

Eight of Diamonds—*Upright.* In its natural position this card is accepted to represent either *the country* or *riches*, as its signification is relatively determined from its surroundings.

In its signification as the *country*, thereby meaning not only a rural district but the characteristics of a country existence, the interpretation of this card boasts a large number of synonyms:

Agriculture; cultivation; field labor; farming; garden; prairie; woods; shades; pleasure; enjoyment; diversion; pastime; amusement; rejuvenation; rural sports; rustic dances; peace; calmness; natural tranquillity; rural life; forests; vales; mountains; flocks and herds; shepherd; shepherdess; moral quietude.

As the synonyms of *riches*, as they are signified by this card in contradistinction to others, we have:

Augmentation of wealth; increase of estate; advancement; prosperity; general success; happiness; goodness; felicity; beauty; embellishment.

Maria D'Andrea's Simple Spells With Playing Cards

Eight of Diamonds—*Reversed*. In this condition the primary signification of the card is *sorrow* and *movement*. The synonyms for *sorrow* are:

Sadness; affliction; displeasure; grief; desolation; mortification; bad humor; melancholy; the blues; hypochondria; vexation; trouble.

But with the word *movement*, we have more trouble to apply its actual signification, as shown in the cards, and therefore the interpreter is left in a great degree to her own judgment, to decipher the connection which should bind the oracle to a specific and intelligent reading.

The most applicable synonyms would therefore be:

To walk; step forward; move about; to contemplate; to propose; to make advances; to undertake; to offer proposals; to promenade; to tender offers; to inaugurate a scheme; to further any claims.

Seven of Diamonds—*Upright*. This is what is most commonly styled the *conversation* card, as its initial and primary signification is *discourse for the present*, while it likewise designates the approaching receipt of *good news*; as the oracle demands, to be secure, proper interpretation.

When used as the *conversation* card, its synonyms are:

Talk; words; matter; tattle; desultory remarks; seasonable language; pleasant gossip; table talk; anecdote.

Secondary to this signification, and in intimate connection, it has oftentimes been employed to denote *designs for the moment*, whether mental or expressed by word of mouth, embracing intent and resolution.

When signifying *news*, the synonyms will be:

Announcement; intelligence; newspaper; advice; advertisement; admonition; warning; teaching; tale telling; history; fables; anecdotal remarks.

Seven of Diamonds—*Reversed*. This card is capable, when emerging reversed, of receiving several interpretations, the general and primary one of which is *birth*, or the origin of a human being, or of matter which has, as its synonyms:

Nativity; origin; creation; source; commencement; principle; primitive; extraction; first coming in of fruits and flowers; prime; early; race; family; house; lineage; posterity; the reason for; cause; premises for argument.

This card frequently designates a *great deal*, or a large quantity, qualifying the value of those cards next to it. For example, should it come before the *ten of spades reversed*, or the *ten of clubs*, it will read a great deal of jealousy, or of money.

Commingled with cards, relating to a public or military official, this one is

Maria D'Andrea's Simple Spells With Playing Cards

taken to signify *declaration*, whose synonyms would consequently be:

Publication; orders; authenticity; approbation; placard; designation; discovery; disclosure; revelation; confession.

King of Hearts—*Upright*. The primary significations of this card are *a blonde man*, *an advocate* and a *man of note*, but its secondary significations are those attached to the state and *legislation*.

As the representative of an individual, this card shows a good, kind-hearted man, of an amorous disposition, rash in his enterprises, and generally hasty and passionate in all his actions.

Coming out as a *blonde man*, it has these synonyms:

Honest man; honesty; probity; equity; arts and sciences.

Considered as a *man of note* or statesman, the synonyms are:

Legislation; legislator; laws; decrees; code; statutes; precepts; commandments; combination; institution; constitution; temperament; complexion; natural and moral law; religious law; civil law; politics; politician; natural right; right of nations; public rights.

King of Hearts—*Reversed*. This card coming out reversed, designates a man of natural light complexion, neither fair nor brown, with dark brown hair and hazel eyes, of an excellent temper, easily imposed upon, credulous, moderately given to love matters, yet addicted to vice and incontinence. Its other primary significations are a *tutor*, or a *man in anger*, possessing vices, the reverse of those good qualities attributed to the card when upright. In this case the synonyms are:

Indignation; agitation; irritation; wrath; rage; fury; frenzy; violence; hatred; aversion; animosity; peril; animadversion; antipathy; resentment; vengeance; affront; outrage; blasphemy; storm; tempest; cruelty; inhumanity; atrocity.

The chief secondary signification of this is a *man in office*, or professional politician, to which are given the following synonyms:

Man of rank; dishonest man; exaction; pillage; injustice; simony; a dishonorable person; a burglar.

Queen of Hearts—*Upright*. This card represents a blonde female, faithful and affectionate, always the dearest friend or nearest relative to the consultant. As such, the synonyms, attached to the primary signification, are of an excellent nature:

Honest woman; virtue; wisdom; honesty.

This card is likewise taken as symbolical of *friendship* in its various phases,

Maria D'Andrea's Simple Spells With Playing Cards

the synonyms of the term being:

Attachment; affection; tenderness; benevolence; kindly relations; fraternity; intimacy; identity in inclinations; agreement; affinity; harmonious correspondence; conformity; sympathy; attraction; cohesion.

Another signification is attached to this card in a secondary capacity as *justice*, with the following synonyms:

Equity; probity; right; rectitude; reason; the law.

A further secondary signification has been bestowed upon this card, under certain influences, when it is gifted with the attributes of *temperance* with these synonyms:

Moderation; discretion; continence; abstinence; patience; calmness; sobriety; frugality; chastity; alleviation; reconciliation; respect; conciliation; mitigation; molification; consolation.

Queen of Hearts—*Reversed*. This card reversed, designates a fair, but not light, woman, with nut-brown hair and grayish eyes, who intervenes to prevent marriage, and intermeddles in all the consultant's affairs generally. It likewise represents either the wife of a man in office, a woman of doubtful character, or a courtesan, a betrayer of honor and of affection. Under this aspect it receives a secondary signification of *dissension*, to which are given synonyms as follows:

Agitations; sedition; conspiracy; rebellion; pride; vanity; seduction; outrage; presumption; disputes; moral wrong; dishonorable proposals.

Jack of Hearts—*Upright*. This card, as a representative one, designates a blonde, unmarried man, learned, good tempered and well favored by fortune. Consequently, when it is drawn by a young woman, and the marriage card comes near it, it portends that she will be united to a person of such a description, and that the union will prove both happy and of long duration.

It likewise designates, primarily, a soldier or a traveler, so that should it come up in your oracle it is interpreted, in a secondary connection, in this sense, and assures that you are on the point of undertaking a journey. If bright cards surround it, the journey will be a prosperous one, but should the *eight of spades* be near it, it will result in illness, and if the *ten of spades* be adjacent, it will be accompanied with tears.

In this secondary capacity it has synonyms as follows:

Road; highway; lane; pathway; a walk; a course; career; promenade; messenger; ways and means; expedient; enterprise; method.

Jack of Hearts—*Reversed*. Should this card come out in the oracle of an

Maria D'Andrea's Simple Spells With Playing Cards

unmarried lady, reversed, it instructs her that her lover or intended husband is a person wooing her for selfish purposes, who, although handsome and accomplished, will make a bad match.

To a married woman, or widow, it is a warning that some unscrupulous individual, under garb of friendship, contemplates her injury, which will be followed by almost immediate desertion, if near the *ace of spades*.

Consequently, in a secondary capacity, it is taken to mean *evil desires* or *longing*, when it has synonyms of this character:

Attraction; passion; flattery; cajolery; adulation; lechery; or declivity; precipice; fall.

Ace of Hearts—*Upright*. The first and primary signification of this card is *the house*, and as such obtains a secondary capacity of a most extensive nature, expressed in the following synonyms:

Household; home; house-keeping; economy; saving; dwelling; domicile; habitation; manor; lodge; lodging; hotel; palace; shop; store; barracks; building; vessel; vase; archives; castle; cabin; cottage; tent; pavilion; inn; hostelry; tavern; religious house; monastery; convent; burial; long home; grave; stable; extraction; family; race; lineage; posterity; ancestry; retreat; asylum.

This card likewise designates a *repast* or *feasting*, when, secondarily, it assumes synonyms of the following nature:

Table; festivity; merry making; nutrition; guests; invitation; host; hilarity; good cheer; abundance; joy; gayety; natural pleasure; domestics; sports and pastimes.

Ace of Hearts—*Reversed*. It primarily designates *forced* or *constrained enjoyment*, but more generally it should be taken for *new acquaintances*, whence is derived a secondary significance of *fresh news*, with these synonyms:

Indication; presentiment; new instructions; fresh knowledge; enlightenment; index; augury; forewarning; fore-knowledge; conjecture; oracle; prognostication; prediction; prophecy; divination; second sight; novelty.

Again this card, reversed, means a *disordered household*, and from this comes the secondary idea of *intestine quarrels*, with the following more prominent synonyms:

Misunderstanding; regret; remorse; repentance; internal agitation; irresolution; uncertainty; family feuds; marriage trouble; domestic strife; dissensions.

At times this card represents *family vices*, or extravagance in household expenditures, or any description of crime or folly which renders home unhappy

Maria D'Andrea's Simple Spells With Playing Cards

and unendurable.

Ten of Hearts—*Upright*. This card ordinarily signifies the *city*, when its secondary capacities are expressed in some one from among the following synonyms:

Metropolis; native land; burgh; village; town; locality; site; town-house; dwelling; habitation; residence; municipality; city government; citizens.

It moreover is accepted to signify *envious people*, as by that term the ancient inhabitants of the rural districts were wont to designate, ironically, dwellers in cities.

Ten of Hearts—*Reversed*. This card most generally signifies *an inheritance*, when its synonyms are:

Succession; legacy; donation; testamentary gifts; dowry; dower; dowager; legitimacy; will; patrimony; heir; transmission; to bequeath; to endow.

It is likewise used to signify *relatives* when its secondary capacity is extended to the widest scope, embracing:

Consanguinity; blood; family; ancestors; father; mother; brother; sister; aunt; uncle; cousin, male or female; Adam and Eve; race; lineage; alliance; relationship; affinity; blood connection; love intrigues.

Another primary signification of this card is *surprise*, generally of a bad origin, with these appropriate synonyms:

Cheat; imposture; knavery; deceit; trickery; mistake; oversight; misunderstanding; trouble; vexation; annoyance; emotion; fright; fear; terror; consternation; astonishment; admiration; alarm; rapture; exhaustion; swooning; fainting; a marvel; phenomenon; miracle; anything wonderful or strange.

Among the ancient cartomancists, this card, with the *nine of hearts*, was regarded as the most difficult of interpretation of any in the pack, but through careful study of the synonyms above given, a true meaning is readily attained.

Nine of Hearts—*Upright*. This card is generally regarded as an augury of good fortune, wealth, happiness and worldly advantage.

Its principal signification is *victory*, whence we derive:

Success; good results; advantage; gain; pomp; triumph; trophies; majesty; show; apparel; baggage; luggage; equipage; attire; furniture; rich goods and wares.

Its next principal one is *union* and *concord*, with the several secondary significations, cognate to them:

Maria D'Andrea's Simple Spells With Playing Cards

Moderation; discretion; continence; temperance; patience; calmness; sobriety; frugality; chastity; harmony; music; musical tastes; perfect happiness.

It moreover designates *labor* and *commerce*, in which capacity its signification is expressed in the synonyms:

Studious; application; work; toil; reflection; observation; meditation; occupation; trade; employment; merchant; clerk; trader; laborer; mercantile pursuits.

Still another signification is *a present*, whence we have:

Gift; generosity; benefit; gratification; service.

Nine of Hearts—*Reversed*. This card means *ennui*, or weariness, with secondary attributes expressed in these synonyms:

Displeasure; discontent; disgust; aversion; inquietude; lack of spirit; listlessness; trivial sorrow; affliction; uneasiness; complaining; want of energy.

It moreover is employed to signify *curiosity*, whence we have the secondary signification of inquisitiveness; a busybody; a marplot and intruder.

Then again an ordinary signification of this card is *obstacle* or *hindrance* with the following synonyms:

Bar; embarrassment; opposition; barrier; contrariety; inconvenience; trouble; difficulty; work; abjection; indisposition; ailment; infirmity; distress; hesitation; vacillation; perplexity; impediment; stumbling-block.

Eight of Hearts—*Upright*. The primary signification of this card is first, a blonde young lady of great natural abilities, gentle manners, lively disposition and personal beauty, for whom we have synonyms:

Honest girl; virtuous girl; modesty; maidenly grace; bashfulness; timidity; retiring disposition; fear of scandal; apprehension; mildness; suavity of temper.

It moreover signifies *success in expectations*, in those enterprises whereupon the consultant has set his heart, with the secondary significations of:

Success; happy issue; fortunate termination; victory; cure; recovery; accomplishment; end of trouble; discontinuance, termination of pains, torment or labor.

Eight of Hearts—*Reversed*. When this card comes into the oracle in a reversed position, and is used as the representative of an individual, it designates an unmarried lady, of a light complexion, with chestnut-brown hair, of a natural good disposition, but spoiled by an assumption of superiority over her companions. From this signification, we have that of *arrogance*, and thence:

Maria D'Andrea's Simple Spells With Playing Cards

Noise; quarreling; dispute; disturbance; difference; contestations; litigation; bickerings; arguments.

But the most general signification of this card reversed is *great joy*, otherwise expressed in these synonyms:

Perfect content; felicity; happiness; rapture; enchantment; ecstasy; entire satisfaction; complete joy; inexpressible pleasure; heavenly inspiration; exhilaration; enthusiasm; the music of the spheres; celestial harmony.

Under other influences this card becomes modified to the signification of the *means of satisfaction*, such as:

Gayety; dancing; the opera; the theater; festival; public rejoicings; family reunions; poetry; romance; joyous visits; pleasant parties; excursions.

Seven of Hearts—*Upright*. When this card emerges in its natural position, its primary signification is that of *thought*, an *arm*, or a *jewel*.

As thought, it has many secondary significations prominent among them those expressed by the synonyms:

The soul; spirit; intelligence; an idea; memory; imagination; conception; comprehension; extension of ideas; designs; intentions; desires; will; resolution; determination; premeditation; meditation; reflection; opinion; sentiment; philosopher; philosophy; wisdom.

This card is sometimes employed to signify *solitude*, when it obtains a secondary signification:

A desert; seclusion; retreat from society; hermitage; exile; banishment; isolation; abandonment.

Seven of Hearts—*Reversed*. When this card comes out reversed, one of its primary significations is a *package*, or bundle, present, new clothes, etc., in accordance with the signification of the cards immediately preceding or following it, which can be easily learned by study.

Nevertheless, its most ordinary signification is *desire*, or a strong longing for, or hankering after, some person or thing; but then again the interpretation is qualified by the cards coming near this one, either before or after; reading from the consultant to the right, by a simple change in position of the cards, *desire* may be changed into *aversion*, and an *attraction* into *repulsion*.

When its signification is *desire*, its synonyms will be:

Wish; now; will; coveting; cupidity; lusting after; concupiscence; unlawful desire; extreme hankering after; jealous; passion for good or bad; illusion; crav-

Maria D'Andrea's Simple Spells With Playing Cards

ing; appetite; a fancy for a thing; decided inclination.

It will be seen that the term *desire* is employed as antagonistic to love, or a holy and righteous phase of passion.

King of Spades—*Upright*. Employed as a representative card, this one designates a man of very dark complexion, with black eyes and hair, passionate and proud, ambitious, and successful in most of his aspirations, but a person whom the reverse of fortune would utterly crush into obscurity.

Divested of this personal and destructive character, this card, when coming upright in an oracle, designates a professional man of eminence, a lawyer, judge, advocate, counselor, senator, practitioner, attorney, confidential agent, jurist, orator, statesman, pleader, diplomat, doctor of laws or in medicine, or a learned physician.

When the consultant be an unmarried lady, this card assures her that her admirer is a man of excessive probity and of honorable intentions, that is, if the *king of diamonds* likewise comes out upright. To a married woman it denotes that her property or honor will be in the keeping of a lawyer or agent of rectitude, who will rescue her from the machinations of enemies or spoliators. To a widow it shows that her second marriage will be to a man of eminence, who will render her after life most happy.

King of Spades—*Reversed*. This card signifies a widower, a man in anger or difficulty, also one given to inebriety. But taken in a general acceptation, this card represents a *wicked man*, and, through induction, *wickedness*. In that case, its secondary significance can be gleaned from the synonyms, used to give expression to it, as follows:

Bad intentioned; innate wickedness; perversity; perfidy; crime; cruelty; inhumanity, and atrocity.

This card is likewise regarded as an unfortunate one, as it forewarns you of the utter wreck of your expectations, wrought by some one of the following causes:

Reverses; prejudice; theft; violence; corruption; elopement; libertinage; debauchery; slander; malice; exposure of secrets; disorder in morals, or calumny.

Queen of Spades—*Upright*. As the repre[Pg 72]sentative of an individual this card designates a dark lady, with dark eyes and black hair, naturally of an open and generous disposition, but who will change her nature through flattery and her position in society. Should she be possessed of beauty, her innocence will be in perpetual danger, and only saved through the exercise of a strong will, or through motives of self-respect.

Maria D'Andrea's Simple Spells With Playing Cards

This card likewise, when emerging upright, designates a *widow*, without respect to color or social position, and is also taken to signify the condition of widowhood, to be interpreted, as the oracle demands, by these synonyms:

Privation; abstinence; absence; scarcity; sterility; poverty; indigence; famine; deprivation.

Frequently this card is employed to denote a *well-founded distrust*, when its secondary significations will be:

Just suspicion; legitimate fear; merited doubts; conjectures; surmises based on fact; conscientious scruples; timidity; bashfulness; reluctance; retirement.

Queen of Spades—*Reversed*. As a representative of an individual, this card, coming out in the oracle reversed in position, denotes a widow, desirous of contracting another marriage. It moreover designates a dark woman of amorous propensities, who does not hesitate to disregard the conventionalities of society.

But as a general thing, this card is assumed to signify a *crafty evil-minded woman*, and can be interpreted as:

Malignity; malice; finesse; artifice; cunning; craft; dissimulation; frolic; pranks; wildness; hypocrisy; bigotry; prudishness; wantonness; shamelessness.

When coming reversed in a consultation upon marriage, this card denotes that difficulties and impediments, generally originating with a female, will be interposed to prevent the desired nuptials.

Jack of Spades—*Upright*. As the representative of an individual, this card, coming out upright, designates a dark complexioned unmarried man, an obliging fellow, who does not hesitate to accommodate his friends at serious disadvantage to himself, if occasion require.

The primary signification of the card is, however, *messenger*, an envoy, or person, charged with bearing of intelligence, most generally employed as a go-between in intrigues, or in a capacity of trust.

Sometimes this card is used to designate a *critic*, or a critical position; a moment of impending danger; an awkward predicament; a decisive instant; an unfortunate situation; a delicate circumstance; a threatened calamity; a crisis; or a perplexing misstep.

Jack of Spades—*Reversed*. This card is one of evil omen to lovers, as it forewarns a betrayal of their secrets, or the exposure of their plans by a corrupt messenger, or through the intervention of some intermeddler.

Its primary signification, when the card is reversed, is that of a *Paul Pry*, or spy, whence we have the secondary ones of inquirer, spectator, watcher, over-

Maria D'Andrea's Simple Spells With Playing Cards

seer, as well as the result of such a man's investigations. Hence applied more generally, the card signifies scrutiny; examination; reports; remarks; notations, and commentaries.

Another secondary signification of this card is *traitor*, from which we readily obtain the following synonyms:

Deception; duplicity; stratagem; disguise; prevarication; disloyalty; breach of trust; conspiracy; tale bearing; imposture; black heartedness; perfidy; falsehood; dissimulation and breach of confidence.

The card is, moreover, used to forewarn lovers that there is danger of their being pursued in event of elopement.

Ace of Spades—*Upright*. This card, coming out in natural position, and intervening between the representative cards of a male and female, relates wholly to love affairs. When accompanied by the *ten of spades* it shows that an intrigue will be accompanied with a deal of sorrow and affliction, and will ultimately end in abandonment under most disastrous circumstances.

One of the primary significations of this card is a *paper* or document, chiefly appertaining to law matters, such as warrants for arrest, writs, subp[oe]nas and legal pleadings.

Another is that of a *ship*, or other means of conveyance by water, particularly when accompanied by the *eight of clubs*, reversed, which betokens the consultant to be on the eve of a sea voyage, or other journey over water of some description.

Ace of Spades—*Reversed*. When in the oracle of a married consultant, this card appears reversed, and near to her representative, its primary signification is *pregnancy*, which in her case can be expressed by the following synonyms:

Conception; maternity; accouchement; childbirth.

From this we derive a secondary signification, applicable to other things, for which we employ correspondent synonyms:

Enlargement; engenderment; fecundity; fertilization; production; composition; increase; augmentation; multiplication; deliverance; parturition; growth; addition.

When reversed and accompanied by the *knave of clubs*, likewise reversed, this card is a premonitor of *death*.

The general secondary signification of this card, when reversed and in the body of the oracle, is a *fall*, whence we have:

Maria D'Andrea's Simple Spells With Playing Cards

Decadence; decline; discouragement; dissipation; ravage; ruin; demolition; destruction; bankruptcy; error; fault; overwhelming sorrows; perdition; an abyss; precipice; gulf; waterfall; disgrace; shame.

Ten of Spades—*Upright*. The general signification of this card is *jealousy*, particularly when accompanied by the *knave of clubs*, which denotes that the consultant, either male or female, is jealous of his or her sweetheart to such a degree that their friendly relations are in danger of being broken off, which will assuredly be the case, if the *nine of spades* should likewise appear in the oracle.

The other primary signification of this card is *tears*, whence we derive a series of secondary significations, as:

Sighs; groans; weeping; complaints; lamentations; griefs; sadness; heart-sickness; affliction; mental agony.

Ten of Spades—*Reversed*. This card, emerging reversed, has, for a general signification, a *loss*, either moral or physical, as the surrounding cards designate. Thus, with the *nine of hearts* intervening between the consultant and this card, it announces that he or she will lose a situation or employment. When it comes preceded by the *ten of clubs*, it betokens the loss of money or valuables. Should the consultant be an unmarried female, and this card comes out reversed near to a knave, likewise reversed, it foretells the ruin of her reputation through calumny. But if in place of one of the knaves the *seven of clubs* should appear, the loss of her character will be brought about through some indiscretion.

Another primary signification of this is *the evening*, as a designation of points of time; still this general term of night has given rise to the application of important secondary significations, of which the sense can be taken from the synonyms:

Shades; obscurely; nocturnal; mysterious; secret; masked; concealed; undiscovered; clandestine; occult; veiled; allegorical; hidden meaning; in secrecy; obscure hints; double meaning; on the sly; to conceal from sight; nocturnal meetings.

Nine of Spades—*Upright*. This is justly regarded to be the most unfortunate card in the pack, as it portends maladies, malignant diseases, family dissensions, defeat in enterprises, constant disappointment, and even death. The primary significations of this card, when in its natural position, are a *priest, mourning* and *disappointment*.

The secondary significations, derived from these sources, are:

From the *priest*: Pastor; church; church services; ritual; sanctity; piety; devotion; religious ceremonies; celibacy.

Maria D'Andrea's Simple Spells With Playing Cards

From *mourning*: Regret; desolation; affliction; sadness; sorrow; calamity; grief; heart-pain; funeral; burial; tomb; grave; church-yard; loss of relatives; wailing.

From *disappointment*: Obstacles; hindrance; delay; disadvantage; contrarieties; misfortunes; suffering.

Nine of Spades—*Reversed*. When this card appears in the oracle reversed its evil influence is augmented two-fold, although its primary significations are modestly expressed as *failure*, *abandonment* and *delay*. The secondary significations are of the most disastrous character.

The synonyms employed for these terms, in this instance, are:

Misery; indigence; famine; necessity; need; poverty; adversity; misfortune; deep affliction; disagreements; correction; chastisement; punishment; reverses; disgrace; imprisonment; detention; arrest; captivity.

But when this card, reversed, comes before the consultant and the *eight of spades*, in the same oracle, it signifies *mortality*, with the following synonyms:

Death; decease; last sigh; end; finish; extinction; annihilation; destruction; utter ruin; abjection; humiliation; prostration; depression; alteration; poisoning; corruption; putrefaction; paralysis; lethargy.

Still in all these sinister aspects the influence of this card can be materially modified, but never counteracted, through intervention of bright cards.

Eight of Spades—*Upright*. This card is ordinarily of bad import, as its primary signification is *sickness*, although it is more generally interpreted as *bad news*. This is its acceptation when preceded by the *knave of spades* or the *knave of diamonds*, or when accompanied by the *ace of diamonds*, and sometimes by the *eight of hearts*, reversed.

When this card signifies *sickness*, its synonyms are:

Illness of the body, soul or mind; bad condition of health or of business; derangement; infirmity; epidemic; gangrene; agony; displeasure; damage; mishap; accidental injury; disaster; indisposition; head-ache; heart-ache; inquietude; melancholy; medicine; remedy; charlatan; empiric; physician; quack; languor.

Sometimes, however, this card is employed to designate *prudence*, whence we have as secondary significations:

Wisdom; reserve; circumspection; reticence; discernment; foresight; presentiment; prediction; divination; prophecy; horoscope; second sight; clairvoyance.

Maria D'Andrea's Simple Spells With Playing Cards

Eight of Spades—*Reversed*. Unlike other cards, the reversal of this one brings with it a modification of its primary significations. Hence, when coming out reversed, it most generally signifies *ambition*, a passion for which we have synonyms as follows:

Desire; wish for; search after; cupidity; jealousy; aspiration; onward; higher; illusion; pride.

Another primary signification bestowed upon this card when emerging reversed, is that of a *nun* or pious woman, whence we derive the secondary signification usually applied to this card and expressed in the synonyms:

Inaction; peace; tranquillity; repose; apathy; inertia; stagnation; rest from labor; pastime, recreation; nonchalance; free from care; idleness; supineness; lethargy; torpidity.

Seven of Spades—*Upright*. As a general exponent of current events, this card is taken to forewarn the consultant of the loss of a valuable friend, whose death will be a source of a great deal of misery. On this account many interpret this card to signify a *coffin*, which may be the case when coming out in close proximity to the *ace of spades* or the *nine of spades*.

Its most accepted primary signification, however, among practical cartomancists, is that of *hope*, whence are derived the secondary ones, expressed in the terms:

Trust; confidence; expectation; desire; inclination; longing after; wish; taste for; whim; humor; fancy.

Seven of Spades—*Reversed*. This card takes a wider and an apparently contradictory scope in its primary significations, when emerging in this manner, being *good advice*, *friendship*, and *indecision*.

From *good advice* we derive, as secondary attributes:

Wise counsels; salutary warnings; news; announcements; advertisements; placards; consultations; admonitions; instruction; advice.

For *friendship* we have the following synonyms:

Attachment; affection; tenderness; benevolence; well wishing; relation; harmony; correspondence; connection; identity; intimacy; agreement with; concordance; concurrence; interest; conformity; sympathy; affinity; attraction; admiration.

For *indecision*, the general synonyms are employed:

Want of resolution; uncertainty; perplexity; inconstancy; frivolity; lightness;

Maria D'Andrea's Simple Spells With Playing Cards

variation; diversity; vacillation; hesitation; versatile; unsteady; changeable; whimsical; flexibility in character; unreliable; undetermined.

King of Clubs—*Upright*. As the representative of an individual, this card designates a man of a complexion neither very dark nor exceedingly light, but a person with medium colored brown hair, grayish eyes, and of an easy, plodding disposition. He will be a man humane, honest and affectionate, given to business, and faithful in all his engagements; he will be personally happy in all his relations in life, as father, husband and citizen, and make everyone happy about him.

The primary significations of this card are, in the first instance, a *friend*, and secondly, a *business man*.

As a *business man* this card has these synonyms:

Merchant; trader; dealer; banker; broker; exchange agent; speculator; calculator; physician; schoolmaster; collegian; geometry; freemason; mathematics; engineer; science; professor.

King of Clubs—*Reversed*. This card, as the representative of an individual, designates a person of middling dark complexion, with chestnut brown hair, who, without being positively wicked, is viciously inclined, and for that reason should not be trusted. Being of a morbid temperament, he will destroy the happiness of others, and render his family miserable through his own viciousness.

A secondary signification is consequently a *vicious man* or *vice* itself, expressed in synonyms as follows:

Vice; defect; default; moral blemish; weakness; moral imperfection; unformed nature; irregularity; flightiness of mind; depravation in manners; libertinism; lewdness; licentious speech; ugliness; deformity; corruption; stench; rottenness.

Queen of Clubs—*Upright*. As a representative of a particular individual, this card designates a brunette lady, of a warm, tender, and sympathetic nature, intellectual, witty and high spirited, of a strongly loving disposition, given to society and social reunions, where she distinguishes herself through her conversational ability.

The most prominent primary signification of this card is *opulence*, which is represented in the following synonyms:

Riches; display; pomp; ostentation; vain show; pageantry; luxury; sumptuousness; assurance; steadiness; confidence; certitude; affirmation; security; hardihood; self-reliance; liberty; frankness; candor; openness; plain-dealing; freedom.

Maria D'Andrea's Simple Spells With Playing Cards

Another signification of this card is a *parley* or *conference*, and is expressed by some of the subjoined synonyms:

Discourse; conversation; talk; communication; colloquy; dissertation; deliberation; discussion; speech; pronunciation; grammar; dictionary; tongue; idiom; jargon; slang; exchange; commerce; trade; traffic; to speak; to confer; to converse; to tattle.

Queen of Clubs—*Reversed*. As a representative of an individual, this card, reversed, denotes a lady whose complexion is brunette, with dark hair and black eyes, but not dark enough to be represented by a *spade*. She will be a woman of warm passions, of fine personal appearance, given to coquetry and dependent more upon her natural charms than education or intellectual training for conquests in her flirtations.

The general signification of this card, reversed, however, is *ignorance* in contradistinction to its attributes when in natural position, and therefore can be interpreted as:

Boorishness; unskillfulness; want of experience; untutored; impertinent.

Jack of Clubs—*Upright*. As a representative of an individual, this card denotes a young man of middling dark complexion, kind, gentle and docile by nature, sedate and domestic in his habits, and studious through inclination. He is a warm friend and faithful admirer.

Coming out in the oracle of a young lady, this card is the representative of her lover, without respect to his color or other qualifications, denoting simply the person indicated.

The primary signification of this card, divested of its representative character, is a *scholar* or lover of knowledge, while its secondary attributes are expressed in the synonyms:

Study; instruction; application; meditation; reflection; labor; toil; work; occupation; apprentice; student; disciple; pupil; master.

Another signification of this card, governed according to its surroundings in the oracle, is *prodigality*, whence are derived synonyms as follows:

Profusion; superfluity; luxury; largess; bounty; sumptuousness; magnificence; liberality; benefits; generosity; charity; benevolence; a crowd; a multitude; depredation; dilapidation; pillage; dissipation.

Jack of Clubs—*Reversed*. As a representative of an individual, this card designates a bachelor, a shade darker, and of a more determined character than the young man above described. It may likewise represent that same young man

Maria D'Andrea's Simple Spells With Playing Cards

in a state of anger or on a sick bed.

Its especial signification, however, is *delirium*, whence we have as secondary attributes or synonyms:

Frenzy; aberration of mind; wandering of the brain; unseated reason; fury; rage; fever; enthusiasm; imbecility; imprudence; distraction; apathy; delirium tremens; intoxication; brain fever.

Ace of Clubs—*Upright*. This card is universally regarded as a most fortunate one, inasmuch as it betokens vast wealth, personal prosperity, physical health, mental tranquillity, marital happiness and longevity.

The principal significations of this card are *a purse of money* and *riches*, whence we have as synonyms:

For *a purse of money*: Sum of money; a present; capital; principal; treasure; bullion; gold and silver wares; opulence; rare; dear; precious; inestimable; of excessive value.

For *riches*: Wealth; health; prosperity; worldly goods; happiness; felicity; amelioration; improvement; benefit; advantage; profit; blessing; favor; grace; plenty; destiny; chance; speculation; good luck.

Ace of Clubs—*Reversed*. When this card emerges to form part of an oracle, in a reversed position, its more popular and current significations are *nobility*, *love* and *a present*, but in a consultation made for a young unmarried lady it signifies that she will unexpectedly unite herself with a man, probably a widower, who will better her fortunes; hence to a female operative this card is a very good omen.

For *nobility* we employ as appropriate synonyms:

A nobleman; a man of consequence; important; great; the eldest son; extended; vast; sublime; renowned; illustrious; powerful; elevated; of good quality; illustration; reputation; consideration; grandeur of soul.

For *love*, a correct interpretation of the oracle may require selection from among the following synonyms:

Passion; inclination; sympathy; affection; allurement; attraction; charm; enticement; disposition; taste for; propensity; admiration; gallantry; complacence for the sex; intrigue; affinity; an affair of gallantry; attachment; devotion.

Ten of Clubs—*Upright*. When this card enters in your oracle it is to apprise you that you will unexpectedly receive a handsome sum of money, a gift or a legacy from some dear friend or near relative. However, at the same time it warns you that your smiles will be intermingled with tears; inasmuch as you will almost simultaneously learn of the death of some person whose love you have cherished.

Maria D'Andrea's Simple Spells With Playing Cards

The chief primary signification of this card is *the future*, whence are derived the following secondary ones:

Hereafter; to come; posthumous; after death; heaven.

Another primary signification is *gain*, which can be interpreted as required, by any of these synonyms:

Advantage; profit; success; grace; favor; benefit; ascendency; power; empire; authority; usurpation; profitable; useful; important; interest; official position.

A more general signification in this card is *money*, from which we have secondary ones of this description:

Wealth; coin; bullion; ingots; gold; silver ware; whiteness; purity; candor; innocence; ingenuity; the moon; purification; twilight; moonlight.

Ten of Clubs—*Reversed*. As a general thing this card, emerging reversed, designates a *lover*, of either gender, unless the *knave of clubs* appears in the oracle of a lady, or the *eight of hearts*, reversed, in that of a gentleman.

Employed in such a signification, we have as synonyms:

In love; gallantry; a gallant; husband; wife; married man; married woman; friend; protector; courtesan; to love; to cherish; to adore; to match; to mate; harmony; concord; suitable; corresponding; in relations with; decency; decorum; regard; seemliness; convenience; vicinity; fitness.

This card is sometimes used to designate *the house*.

Nine of Clubs—*Upright*. The general primary signification of this card, when employed as a measure of time, is *the present*, whence we have as synonyms:

At the instant; actually; now; presently; suddenly; unexpectedly; upon the spot; momentarily; at hand.

The second primary signification of this card is an *effect*, whence are derived the secondary ones of this nature:

For sure; with certainty; in consequence; result; evidence; conviction; conclusion; will happen; event; to finish; to execute; household goods; furniture; bonds; personal estate; jewelry; movable goods.

This card has another primary signification, *indiscretion*, from which are derived the secondary meanings, as follows:

Want of foresight; imprudent; rash; headlong; with precipitation; thoughtlessly; impulsively; suddenly; disorder; confusion; misconduct; want of reflection; chaos; disgrace; without restraint; dissipation; libertinage; discordance; in-

Maria D'Andrea's Simple Spells With Playing Cards

harmonious; moral ruin.

Nine of Clubs—*Reversed*. This card, reversed, is most usually employed to denote that the consultant, in whose oracle it appears, will be the recipient of a *present*, but as to its value and its nature the surrounding cards must determine. The card consequently may represent:

Gift; presentation; memorial; offering; testimonial; a gratification; service; offer of money; thanksgiving.

Another signification of this card when coming out reversed, is *gambling*, but as this is a serious moral offense, great care should be exercised to study its application.

From *gambling* are derived these secondary meanings:

Games of chance; lottery; luck; card playing; any fortuitous circumstance; by accident; destiny; human life; cards; dice; money games; disreputable company.

Eight of Clubs—*Upright*. As a representative of an individual, this card designates a brunette, unmarried lady, remarkable for her personal attractions, of a mild and tractable nature, who, should she not possess beauty, will win admiration from her accomplishments and demeanor, as well as from her sincerity and virtue.

As a general thing this card signifies *the art of pleasing*, or, as it is more appropriately styled, *a virtuous girl*, in which connection, its meaning is expressed in the synonyms:

A virgin; chaste; modest; virtuous; genteel; becoming; decent; decorous; suitable; befitting; civil; kind; courteous; polished; polite; well bred; accomplished; condescending; meek; hospitable; good manners.

Eight of Clubs—*Reversed*. As an individual's representative, this card, when reversed, denotes a middling dark complexioned unmarried woman, with dark chestnut hair, and eyes nearly approaching black in color. She will be vain of her personal charms, and make little account of the world's opinion should her own desires be gratified.

The primary signification of this card is *removal* or *departure*, and can be appropriately expressed in the following synonyms:

Moving; to move; change of residence; at a distance; remote; absence; separation; dispersion; going aside; out of the way; ramble; excursion; digression; flight; to discard; disdain; repugnance; aversion; incompatibility; opposition; division; rupture, and antipathy.

Maria D'Andrea's Simple Spells With Playing Cards

This card, reversed, has moreover the signification of *indecorum*, which can be used in these different senses:

Inhospitable; ill bred; discourteous; bad manners; immodest; unchaste; insincere; boorish; brazen faced; slovenly; a virago; a tartar; a wanton.

Seven of Clubs—*Upright*. The principal primary signification of this card is a *trifle in money*, but which, however, has been amplified to designate *economy*, or the art of spending very little money to the best advantage. Consequently from this source we have the following synonyms:

Good behavior; wise administration of affairs; foresight; discretion; order; regularity; household virtues; good management; wisdom; happiness; prosperity.

This card likewise signifies *company* or *sociability*, in which connection it can be taken to denote:

Association; an assembly; a gathering; family party; friendly intercourse; pleasant relations; harmless pastimes; domestic recreations; balls; concerts; theater.

Still, its most important signification is a *child*. From this physical object the secondary meanings of this card are extended to designate the characteristics of childhood applied to after life. Hence the synonyms of this signification are:

Infancy; childhood; puerility; frivolity; weakness; dependency; abasement; humiliation; depression; humble; abject; minute; small; diminutive; helpless.

Seven of Clubs—*Reversed*. As a general thing this card reversed has the signification of *embarrassment* or *impediment*, and, taken in this light, its meanings, as applied to the exigencies of a correct interpretation of the consultation, will be found in some one of these synonyms:

Hindrance; entanglement; clog; fuss; intricacy; confusion; exigency; disorder; distress; to make work; to come to a stand; to perplex; to puzzle; to obstruct; to delay; to block up; to choke up; to stop up; to stifle; hurry; bustle; in a fix; in perplexity; at a loss.

It must be borne in mind that this card, when signifying a child, may come out either upright or reversed.

GROUPS OF CARDS

All Four, Any Three and Any Two of a Kind, that Come Out in the Deal, Either Upright or Reversed, to the RIGHT of the Consultant—Their Meanings.

Four Kings—Removal.

Maria D'Andrea's Simple Spells With Playing Cards

Four Queens—Great assemblage of ladies.

Four Jacks—An illness.

Four Aces—A great surprise.

Four Tens—An affair of justice.

Four Nines—An agreeable surprise.

Four Eights—A reverse.

Four Sevens—Intrigue.

Three Kings—Consultation.

Three Queens—Female deceit.

Three Jacks—A trifling dispute.

Three Aces—Paltry success.

Three Tens—Change in social position.

Three Nines—Petty results.

Three Eights—Unfortunate marriage.

Three Sevens—Pain in the limbs. Contrariness.

Two Kings—Petty counsel.

Two Queens—Friends.

Two Jacks—Inquietude.

Two Aces—Deception.

Two Tens—Change.

Two Nines—A little money.

Two Eights—A new acquaintance.

Two Sevens—Trifling news.

All Four, Any Three and Any Two of a Kind, that Come Out in the Deal, Either Upright or Reversed, to the LEFT of the Consultant—Their Meanings.

Four Kings—Celerity in business matters.

Four Queens—Bad company.

Four Jacks—Privation.

Maria D'Andrea's Simple Spells With Playing Cards

Four Aces—Disagreeable surprise.

Four Tens—An occurrence, an event.

Four Nines—Disagreeable surprise.

Four Eights—Error.

Four Sevens—An unjust man.

Three Kings—Commerce.

Three Queens—Friendly repast.

Three Jacks—Idleness.

Three Aces—Misconduct.

Three Tens—Want.

Three Nines—Imprudence.

Three Eights—A play.

Three Sevens—Great joy.

Two Kings—You have projects.

Two Queens—Occupation.

Two Jacks—Company.

Two Aces—Enemies.

Two Tens—To be in expectation.

Two Nines—Profit.

Two Eights—You will be crossed.

Two Sevens—A new acquaintance will criticize you.

COMBINATIONS OF TWO CARDS

Coming Together in the Deal—Their Meanings—"Upright" Unless Otherwise Stated—First Card Named is the Lefthand One of the Two.

Seven of diamonds and seven of spades, both reversed—A quarrel.

Seven and queen of diamonds, both reversed—A quarrel.

Nine of diamonds and eight of hearts—A journey.

Ace of spades reversed and nine of hearts—Despair.

Maria D'Andrea's Simple Spells With Playing Cards

Nine of diamonds and seven of spades reversed—Delay.

Eight of clubs and ace of clubs reversed—Declaration of love.

Eight of diamonds and eight of spades—A difficulty between two persons.

Ten of clubs reversed and eight of diamonds—You will go out of your way to reach your house.

Seven of spades and seven of hearts, both reversed—Security, independence; deliverance from some trouble.

Ace of hearts and ace of spades reversed—Distrust.

King and ace of hearts, both reversed—Loan office or pawnbroker's.

King of spades reversed and ace of hearts—Palace.

Ten of diamonds and ten of spades reversed—Anger.

Nine of spades reversed and nine of diamonds—Great delay.

King of hearts reversed and ace of hearts—Banquet hall; festivity.

Seven of hearts and seven of spades reversed—You are undecided regarding a certain person.

Ten and ace of diamonds—You will send a letter to a foreign city.

Eight of clubs reversed and ten of diamonds—Departure for a distant foreign city.

Jack and ace of spades—Second marriage.

Ace of spades and seven of spades reversed—Lawsuit.

Jack of hearts and jack of spades reversed—Uneasiness about politics.

Ace of clubs and seven of diamonds reversed—A deal of money.

Queen of spades and eight of hearts—A blonde widow.

Ace of hearts reversed and jack of diamonds—Someone is waiting for you.

Ace of hearts and ten of diamonds—A blow.

Queen of diamonds reversed and king of diamonds—A handsome stranger.

Jack of diamonds reversed and ace of spades—You await somebody.

King of hearts reversed and ace of hearts—Ballroom.

Ace and ten of clubs—A sum of money.

Ace of spades reversed and queen of clubs—Injustice.

Maria D'Andrea's Simple Spells With Playing Cards

Ace of hearts reversed and ten of hearts—Surprise at the house.

Ten of clubs and ten of spades, both reversed—Loss of money.

Ten of spades and ten of clubs, both reversed—Money at night.

Seven of clubs and seven of hearts—You think of silver.

Seven of hearts and ten of diamonds—You will have gold.

Ten of diamonds and ace of clubs reversed—Present of gold.

Ten of clubs and ten of hearts—Surprise of money.

Ace of hearts and seven of diamonds reversed—Words at the house.

Seven of spades and ace of clubs, both reversed—Declaration of love.

Eight of diamonds and seven of hearts reversed—You desire to take a walk.

Ace of clubs reversed and ten of hearts—A love surprise.

Ten of spades and seven of hearts reversed—You will receive a shock.

Seven of hearts and ten of spades reversed—You will lose a small object.

King and ace of hearts, both reversed—Gaming house. Stock exchange.

King and queen of clubs—Married couple.

Ten of diamonds and eight of hearts reversed—Unexpected voyage.

Jack of diamonds reversed and queen of diamonds—A domestic and home-loving woman.

Eight of diamonds and eight of spades—Sickness.

Eight of diamonds and eight of clubs—Moving to the country.

Ace of clubs and ten of spades, both reversed—Jealousy in love.

Eight of diamonds and seven of spades reversed—Hesitation about going to the country.

Queen of clubs and seven of diamonds reversed—Discussion.

Seven of spades reversed and seven of hearts—You think of being someone's friend.

Ace of spades reversed and nine of diamonds—You will experience a delay with some paper.

Ace of hearts and jack of clubs—Flattery.

Eight of clubs reversed and eight of hearts—Great affection.

Maria D'Andrea's Simple Spells With Playing Cards

Seven of diamonds and seven of clubs, both reversed—A great deal of embarrassment.

Seven of spades reversed and nine of diamonds—Certain delay or separation.

King of hearts reversed and ace of hearts—Convent.

King and nine of spades, both reversed—Want.

King and queen of hearts—A married couple in good society.

King of hearts reversed and ace of hearts—Court of justice.

King of diamonds and eight of clubs—Robber.

Eight of clubs and king of diamonds—Theft.

King and nine of spades, both reversed—Unjust accusation.

King of diamonds reversed and ace of clubs—A rich countryman.

Jack of diamonds reversed and jack of spades—Strange young man.

Ace of spades and jack of diamonds, both reversed—Someone expects you.

King of hearts reversed and ace of hearts—Large house, hotel.

Queen and ace of spades, both reversed—Infidelity.

Ace of spades reversed and king of hearts—Hospital.

Ace of clubs and ace of spades, both reversed—Imprisonment.

King and queen of clubs—Man and wife.

King of hearts reversed and ace of hearts—Government house; campground.

Ace of hearts and eight of hearts reversed—Money due.

Ace of clubs reversed and ace of diamonds—Love-letter.

Queen of hearts and nine of spades reversed—A lady in mourning.

King and queen of diamonds, both reversed—A country lady and gentleman.

Ace of hearts and queen of clubs reversed—Injustice.

Maria D'Andrea's Simple Spells With Playing Cards

A WORD OF ADVICE.

It will be found of material assistance to the complete understanding of each of the following methods of telling fortunes to have in your hands a 32-card pack as you read, and to carefully follow out the details with the exact cards mentioned in the text. We strongly recommend this plan to the student who desires to become an adept in the art.

SPECIAL NOTE.

In all the following methods the 32-card pack is used, which consists of the ace, king, queen, jack, ten, nine, eight and seven only of each suit, and usually the extra Consultant card to represent the person consulting the cards.

When about to consult the oracle, the cards should be arranged in the following manner before shuffling: King, queen, jack, ace, ten, nine, eight and seven of each suit. This precaution should be taken for every consultation, whether for yourself or for another person, as without this the permutation may chance not to be perfect.

DEALING THE CARDS BY THREES

The pack of thirty-two selected cards is taken, and a card is selected to represent the dealer, supposing he is making the essay on his own behalf; if not, it must represent the person for whom he is acting. In doing this, if the Consultant card be not used, it is necessary to remember that the card chosen should be according to the complexion of the chooser. King or queen of diamonds for a very fair person; king or queen of hearts for one rather dark; clubs for one darker still; and spades only for one very dark indeed. The card chosen also loses its signification, and simply becomes the representative of a dark or fair man or woman as the case may be. This point having been settled, the cards are shuffled, and either cut by the dealer or for him (according to whether he is acting for himself or another person), the left hand being used. That done, they are turned up by threes,

Maria D'Andrea's Simple Spells With Playing Cards

and every time two of the same suit are found in these triplets, such as two hearts, two clubs, etc., the highest card is withdrawn and placed on the table in front. If the triplet chance to be all the same suit, the highest card is still to be the only one withdrawn, but should it consist of three of the same value, such as three kings, etc., they are all to be appropriated. If after having turned up the cards, three by three, six have been able to be withdrawn, there will remain twenty-six, which are shuffled and cut, and again turned up by threes, acting precisely as before, until thirteen, fifteen or seventeen cards have been obtained. The number must always be uneven, and the card representing the person consulting must be amongst the number; if not, it must be drawn out and put at the end.

Say that the person whose fortune is being read is a lady, represented by the queen of hearts, and that fifteen cards are obtained and laid out in the form of a semi-circle in the order they were drawn: The seven of clubs, the ten of diamonds, the seven of hearts, the jack of clubs, the king of diamonds, the nine of diamonds, the ten of hearts, the queen of spades, the eight of hearts, the jack of diamonds, the queen of hearts, the nine of clubs, the seven of spades, the ace of clubs, the eight of spades. The cards having been considered, there are found among them two queens, two jacks, two tens, three sevens, two eights and two nines. It is therefore possible to announce:—"The two queens are supposed to signify the re-union of friends; the two jacks, that there is mischief being made between them. These two tens, a change, which, from one of them being between two sevens, will not be effected without some difficulty; the cause of which, according to these three sevens, will be illness. However, these two nines can promise some small gain; resulting, so say these two eights, from a love affair."

Seven cards are now counted from right to left, beginning with the queen of hearts, who represents the lady consulting the cards. The seventh being the king of diamonds, the following may be said: "You often think of a fair man in uniform."

The next seventh card (counting the king of diamonds as one) proves to be the ace of clubs: "You will receive from him some very joyful tidings; he, besides, intends making you a present."

Count the ace of clubs as one, and proceeding to the next seventh card, the queen of spades: "A widow is endeavoring to injure you on this very account; and (the seventh card counting the queen as one being the ten of diamonds) the annoyance she gives you will oblige you to either take a journey or change your residence; but (this ten of diamonds being imprisoned between two sevens) your journey or removal will meet with some obstacle."

On proceeding to count as before, calling the ten of diamonds one, the seventh card will be found to be the queen of hearts herself, the person consulting; therefore, the conclusion may be stated as: "But this you will overcome of your-

Maria D'Andrea's Simple Spells With Playing Cards

self, without needing anyone's aid or assistance."

The two cards at either extremity of the half circle are now taken, which are respectively the eight of spades and seven of clubs, and may be read: "A sickness which will result in your receiving a small sum of money."

Repeat the same maneuver, which brings together the ace of clubs and the ten of diamonds:

"Good news, which will make you decide on taking a journey, destined to prove a very happy one, and which will occasion you to receive a sum of money."

The next cards united, being the seven of spades and the seven of hearts, you say:

"Tranquillity and peace of mind, followed by slight anxiety, quickly followed by love and happiness."

Then come the nine of clubs and the jack of clubs: "You will certainly receive money through the exertions of a clever dark young man."

Queen of hearts and king of diamonds: "Which comes from a fair man in uniform. This recontre announces great happiness in store for you, and the complete fulfillment of your wishes."

Jack of diamonds and nine of diamonds: "Although this happy result will be delayed some time through a fair young man, not famed for his delicacy."

Eight of hearts and ten of hearts: "Love, joy and triumph."

"The queen of spades, who remains alone, is the widow endeavoring to injure you, and finds herself deserted by all her friends."

The cards that have been in use are now gathered up and shuffled and cut with the left hand. They are then made into three packs by dealing one to the left, one to the middle, and one to the right; a fourth is laid aside to form "a surprise." Then the cards are continued to be dealt to each of the three packs in turn until their number is exhausted, when it will be found that the left hand and middle packs contain each five cards, while the one on the right hand consists of only four.

The person consulting is now asked to select one of the three packs. Supposing this to be the middle one, and that the cards comprising it are the jack of diamonds, the king of diamonds, the seven of spades, the queen of spades, the seven of clubs; recollecting the previous instructions regarding the individual and the supposed relative signification of the cards, they may be easily interpreted as follows: "The jack of diamonds—a fair young man possessed of no delicacy of feeling, seeks to injure—the king of diamonds—a fair man in uniform—seven of

Maria D'Andrea's Simple Spells With Playing Cards

spades—and will succeed in causing him some annoyance—the queen of spades—at the instigation of a spiteful woman—seven of clubs—but by means of a small sum of money matters will be easily arranged."

The left hand pack is next taken up, which is "for the house" the former one having been for the lady herself.

Supposing it to consist of the queen of hearts, the jack of clubs, the eight of hearts, the nine of diamonds and the ace of clubs, they would be read thus: "Queen of hearts—the lady whose fortune is being told is or soon will be in a house—jack of clubs—where she will meet with a dark young man, who—eight of hearts—will entreat her assistance to forward his interests with a fair girl—nine of diamonds—he having met with delay and disappointment—ace of clubs—but a letter will arrive announcing the possession of money, which will remove all difficulties."

The third pack is "for those who do not expect it," and will be composed of four cards: the ten of hearts, the nine of clubs, eight of spades, and ten of diamonds: "The ten of hearts—an unexpected piece of good fortune and great happiness—nine of clubs—caused by an unlooked for legacy—eight of spades—which joy may be followed by a short sickness—ten of diamonds—the result of a fatiguing journey."

There now remains on the table only the card intended for "the surprise." This, however, must be left untouched, the other cards gathered up, shuffled, cut, and again laid out in three packs, not forgetting at the first deal to add a card to "the surprise." After the different packs have been duly examined and explained as before described, they must again be gathered up, shuffled, etc., indeed the whole operation repeated, after which, the three cards forming "the surprise" are examined, and supposing them to be the seven of hearts, the jack of clubs and the queen of spades, they are to be thus interpreted: "Seven of hearts—pleasant thoughts and friendly intentions—jack of clubs—of a dark young man—queen of spades—relative to a malicious dark woman, who will cause him much unhappiness."

DEALING THE CARDS BY FIVES

Shuffle the 32-card pack thoroughly and cut it twice with the left hand, placing the first cut face downward at the right hand and the second on the left.

Now take off the top card of the middle package and place it aside, and repeat the shuffling and cutting of the balance in a precisely similar manner, and again remove the top card of the middle package. Repeat shuffling, cutting and discarding until you have in this way taken out five cards. This done, examine if the Consultant be among the number of cards taken from the pack. If it be, shuffle the five cards well, and then deal them in a row, turning their faces up from right

Maria D'Andrea's Simple Spells With Playing Cards

to left in this manner:

> 5, 4, 3, 2, 1

and proceed to read them from the same direction.

If the Consultant be not found among the five cards drawn as above, take it from the pack and substitute it for one taken by chance from the five cards after shuffling them thoroughly, faces down, so that the card to be discarded shall not be recognized. After placing the Consultant among the other four cards, shuffle well and deal as directed, and you have your oracle of five cards for consultation and explanation, and among which the Consultant will appear in its proper position.

As an example, let us say that the five cards obtained are, from right to left, as follows: Ten of hearts, ten of clubs, Consultant, eight of clubs reversed and ten of diamonds.

The Consultant having behind him the eight of clubs near to the ten of diamonds, these two cards announce to him his residence at a distance in a foreign city, and the two tens which are found placed behind him notifies that he is about to quit his house (ten of clubs) and the city (ten of hearts) where he now lives.

DEALING THE CARDS BY SEVENS

After having shuffled the pack of thirty-two selected cards either cut them yourself or, if acting for another person, let that person cut them, taking care to use the left hand. Then count seven cards, beginning with the one lying on the top of the pack. The first six are useless, so put them aside, and retain only the seventh, which is to be placed face uppermost on the table before you. Repeat this three times more, then shuffle and cut the cards you have thrown on one side, together with those remaining in your hand, and tell them out in sevens as before, until you have thus obtained twelve cards. It is however indispensable that the Consultant card or one representing the person whose fortune is being told should be among the number; therefore the whole operation must be recommenced in case of it not having made its appearance. Your twelve cards being now spread out before you in the order in which they have come to hand, you may begin to explain them as described in the manner of dealing the cards in threes—always bearing in mind both their individual and relative signification. Thus, you first count the cards by sevens, beginning with the one representing the person for whom you are acting, going from right to left. Then take the two cards at either extremity of the line or half-circle, and unite them, and afterwards form the three heaps or packs and "the surprise" precisely as we have before described. Indeed, the only difference between this and the three card method is the manner in which the cards are obtained.

Maria D'Andrea's Simple Spells With Playing Cards

DEALING BY FIFTEENS

After the cards have been well shuffled and cut, they are dealt out in two packs containing sixteen cards in each. The person consulting is desired to choose one of them; the first card is laid aside to form "the surprise," the other fifteen are turned up and ranged in a half circle before the dealer, going from left to right, being placed in the order in which they come to hand. If the card representing the person consulting be not among them the cards must be all gathered up, shuffled, cut, and dealt as before, and this must be repeated till the missing card makes its appearance in the pack chosen by the person it represents. They are explained, first, by interpreting the meaning of any pairs, triplets, or quartettes among them; then by counting them in sevens, going from right to left, and beginning with the card representing the person consulting, and lastly, by taking the cards at either extremity of the line, and pairing them. This being done, the fifteen cards are gathered up, shuffled, cut, and dealt so as to form three packs of five cards each. From each of these the topmost card is withdrawn and placed on the one laid aside for "the surprise," thus forming four packs of four cards each.

The person consulting is desired to choose one of these packs for herself or for himself as the case may be. This is turned up, and the four cards it contains are spread out from left to right, the individual and relative signification ascribed to them being duly explained. In like manner the pack on the left, which will be "for the house," is used; then the third one, "for those who do not expect it;" and lastly, "the surprise."

In order to make the meaning perfectly clear another example is given. It is supposed that the pack for the person consulting consists of the jack of hearts, the ace of diamonds, the queen of clubs and the eight of spades reversed.

It will be easy to interpret them as follows: "The jack of hearts—a gay young bachelor—the ace of diamonds—who has written, or who will very soon write a letter—the queen of clubs—to a dark woman—eight of spades reversed—to make proposals to her, which will not be accepted." On looking back to the list of significations, it will be found to run thus:

Jack of Hearts—A gay young bachelor who thinks only of pleasure.

Ace of Diamonds—A letter, soon to be received.

Queen of Clubs—An affectionate woman, but quick tempered and touchy.

Eight of Spades—If reversed, a marriage broken off, or offer refused.

It will thus be seen that each card forms, as it were, a phrase, from an assemblage of which nothing but a little practice is required to form complete sentences. Of this a further example will be given by interpreting the signification of

Maria D'Andrea's Simple Spells With Playing Cards

the three other packs.

"For the house" is supposed to consist of the queen of hearts, the jack of spades reversed, the ace of clubs and the nine of diamonds, which are supposed to read thus: "The queen of hearts—a fair woman, mild and amiable in disposition—jack of spades reversed—will be deceived by a dark, ill bred young man—the ace of clubs—but she will receive some good news, which will console her—nine of diamonds—although it is probable that this news may be delayed."

The pack "for those who do not expect it," consists of the queen of diamonds, the king of spades, the ace of hearts reversed, and the seven of spades: "The queen of diamonds—a mischief-making woman—the king of spades—in league with a dishonest lawyer—ace of hearts reversed—they will hold a consultation—seven of spades—but the harm they will do will soon be repaired."

Last comes "the surprise," formed by, it is supposed, the jack of clubs, the ten of diamonds, the queen of spades and the nine of spades, of which the supposed interpretation is: "The jack of clubs—a clever, enterprising young man—ten of diamonds—about to undertake a journey—queen of spades—for the purpose of visiting a widow—nine of spades—but one or both their lives will be endangered."

THE TWENTY-ONE CARD METHOD

After the thirty-two cards have been shuffled and cut with the left hand, the first eleven are withdrawn from the pack and laid on one side. The remainder—twenty-one in all—are to be again shuffled and cut, that being done, the topmost card is laid on one side to form "the surprise," and the remaining twenty are ranged before the dealer in the order in which they come to hand. If the card representing the person consulting be not among them, one must be withdrawn from the eleven useless ones placed at the right extremity of the row, where it represents the missing card, no matter what it may really be. Let us suppose that the person wishing to make the essay is an officer in the army, and consequently represented by the king of diamonds, and that the twenty cards ranged in front of you are: Queen of diamonds, king of clubs, ten of hearts, ace of spades, queen of hearts reversed, seven of spades, jack of diamonds, ten of clubs, king of spades, eight of diamonds, king of hearts, nine of clubs, jack of spades reversed, seven of hearts, ten of spades, king of diamonds, ace of diamonds, seven of clubs, nine of hearts, ace of clubs. You now proceed to examine the cards as they lay, and perceiving that all the four kings are there, you can predict that great rewards await the person consulting you, and that he will gain great dignity and honor. The two queens, one of them reversed, announce the reunion of two sorrowful friends; the three aces, foretell good news; the two jacks, one of them reversed, danger; the three tens, improper conduct.

Maria D'Andrea's Simple Spells With Playing Cards

You now begin to explain the cards, commencing with the first on the left hand: "The queen of diamonds is a mischief-making, under-bred woman—the king of clubs—endeavoring to win the affections of a worthy and estimable man—ten of hearts—over whose scruples she will triumph—ace of spades—the affair will make some noise—queen of hearts reversed—and greatly distress a charming fair woman who loves him—seven of spades—but her grief will not be of long duration. Jack of diamonds—an unfaithful servant—ten of clubs—will make away with a considerable sum of money—king of spades—and will be brought to trial—eight of diamonds—but saved from punishment through a woman's agency. King of hearts—a fair man of liberal disposition—nine of clubs—will receive a large sum of money—jack of spades reversed—which will expose him to the malice of a dark youth of coarse manners. Seven of hearts—pleasant thoughts, followed by—ten of spades—great chagrin—king of diamonds—await a man in uniform, who is the person consulting me—ace of diamonds—but a letter he will speedily receive—seven of clubs—containing a small sum of money—nine of hearts—will restore his good spirits—ace of clubs—which will be further augmented by some good news." Now turn up "the surprise" which it is supposed will prove the ace of hearts, "a card that is taken to predict great happiness, caused by a love letter, but which, making up the four aces, is said to show that this sudden joy will be followed by great misfortunes."

The cards are now gathered up, shuffled, cut, and formed into three packs, at the first deal one being laid aside to form "the surprise." By the time they are all dealt out it will be found that the two first packets are each composed of seven cards, whilst the third contains only six. The person consulting is desired to select one of these, which is taken up and spread out from left to right, being explained as before described. The cards are again gathered up, shuffled, cut, formed into three packs, one card being dealt to "the surprise," and then proceeding as before. The whole operation is once more repeated, then the three cards forming "the surprise" are taken up and their interpretation given.

No matter how the cards are dealt, whether by threes, fives, sevens, fifteens or twenty-one, when those lower than the jack predominate it is considered to foretell success. If clubs are the most[Pg 120] numerous, they are supposed to predict gain, considerable fortune, etc. If picture cards, dignity and honor; hearts, gladness, good news; spades, death or sickness.

Maria D'Andrea's Simple Spells With Playing Cards

THE WAY TO TELL A FORTUNE

Illustrating the 21-card deal and the expert fortune-teller's method of constructing a complete and connected reading of the same, which you are advised to carefully consider, as a guide for your own use in delivering an intelligent, interesting and coherent oracle in all cases where you are rendering an interpretation for others.

A man asks the question:

Shall I Marry the Woman I Love?

The fortune-teller turns the cards by the 21-card method, with the resultant layout as shown in the picture, and proceeds to read the gentleman's answer in the following language:

You desire to learn, sir, whether you will marry the young lady to whom you are now paying your addresses? You inform me that the lady is a blonde; still it is necessary for me to inform you that in order to be able to foresee whether or not the marriage be accomplished according to your wishes, I am compelled to select as a representative card of your future wife, a lady of your own color, for such a one is necessary for the oracle, otherwise our labors go for nothing. You, sir, are a middling dark man, and therefore would come up as a *club*; as a representative card of your beloved we will take the *queen of clubs*, as of your own complexion.

Now, sir, having performed our deal and arranged the oracle, permit me, in the first place, to call your attention to the fact that you stand represented by the *knave of clubs*, and in the next to observe your position in the oracle.

The *eight of hearts* coming as it does in company with the *eight of clubs*, gives me satisfactory information that you entertain for the young lady a most profound and honorable sentiment of affection, which it appears to me she reciprocates with a no less degree of intensity. I have chosen to designate your beloved by the *queen of clubs*, and she is doubtlessly a personage well worthy of your love, as the *eight of diamonds*, coming before her in conjunction with the *ace of hearts*, demonstrates her to be a lady of wisdom, intelligence and prudence. Ob-

Maria D'Andrea's Simple Spells With Playing Cards

serve, moreover, that the *nine of hearts* intervenes between you both, but is placed nearest the lady. This card predicts a union, which is much desired by her, while on your part you regard your intended with a spirit of admiration bordering almost upon adoration. Such a union will assuredly be followed by domestic happiness, by peace and concord in your domestic circle, by a reign of harmony within your household.

I assure you, sir, that, scrutinizing this oracle from every aspect, I fail to perceive any obstacle which can interpose to prevent your contemplated marriage. On the other hand, the prognostications are decidedly in its favor, for you will be pleased to notice that the *eight of hearts* and the *eight of clubs*, coming up side by side, and between you and your intended, predict a success. Remark more, that there are *three tens* at your back, which denotes a change in your estate or an alteration in your manner of life and social position.

The presence of the *queen of hearts* in immediate vicinity to the *seven of diamonds*, indicates not only the receipt of pleasant intelligence from a relative able to give you assistance, but permanent prosperity should you continue in her good graces. I perceive, likewise, from the *seven of hearts*, that you are at this moment thinking of visiting your intended father-in-law, formally to demand the hand of his daughter.

Do not hesitate, my dear sir, to do so, for you will risk nothing by such an act of courtesy, as it will be crowned with the most happy results. There can be no doubt on that head, as the presence of the *king*, *queen* and *knave of hearts*, coming almost together, and blended with your new estate, assure you of the respect and esteem of the family. True, the young lady entertains such affection (*seven of spades*) for her parent that when she comes to be separated (*nine of diamonds*) from him upon marriage (*king of diamonds*) the native impulse of her heart will cause her to shed tears (*ten of spades*) at the thought (*seven of hearts*) of leaving her paternal roof (*ace of hearts*).

And now, sir, your surprise. It is a letter (*ace of diamonds*), which, placed upon the last card to the left, which is the *king of clubs*, announces to you that you will be surprised through receipt of a most gratifying epistle from your intended father-in-law in relation to your approaching marriage.

THE ITALIAN METHOD

Take the pack of thirty-two selected cards, shuffle them well, and either cut or have them cut for you, according to whether you are acting for yourself or another person. Turn up the cards by threes, and when the triplet is composed of cards of the same suit, lay it aside; when of three different suits, pass it by without withdrawing any of the three; but when composed of two of one suit and one of

Maria D'Andrea's Simple Spells With Playing Cards

another, withdraw the higher card of the two. When you have come to the end of the pack, gather up all the cards except those you have withdrawn; shuffle, cut, and again turn up by threes. Repeat this operation until you have obtained fifteen cards, which must then be spread out before you, from left to right, in the order in which they come to hand.

Care must, however, be taken that the card representing the person making the essay is among them; if not, the whole operation must be recommenced until the desired result is obtained. We will suppose it to be some dark lady—represented by the queen of clubs—who is anxious to make the attempt for herself, and that the cards are laid out in the following order, from left to right: Ten of diamonds, queen of clubs, eight of hearts, ace of diamonds, ten of hearts, seven of clubs, king of spades, nine of hearts, jack of spades, ace of clubs, seven of spades, ten of spades, seven of diamonds, ace of spades, jack of hearts.

On examining them, you will find that there are three aces among them, announcing good news; but, as they are at some distance from each other, that the tidings may be some time before they arrive.

The three tens denote that the conduct of the person consulting the cards has not been always strictly correct. The two jacks are enemies, and the three sevens predict an illness, caused by them.

You now begin to count five cards, beginning with the queen of clubs, who represents the person consulting you. The fifth card, being the seven of clubs, announces that the lady will soon receive a small sum of money. The next fifth card proving to be the ace of clubs, signifies that this money will be accompanied by some very joyful tidings. Next comes the ace of spades, promising complete success to any projects undertaken by the person consulting the cards; then the eight of hearts, followed at the proper interval by the king of spades, showing that the good news will excite the malice of a dishonest lawyer; but the seven of spades coming next, announces that the annoyance he can cause will be of short duration, and that a gay, fair young man—the jack of hearts—will soon console her for what she has suffered. The ace of diamonds tells that she will soon receive a letter from this fair young man—the nine of hearts—announcing a great success—ten of spades—but this will be followed by some slight chagrin—ten of diamonds—caused by a journey—ten of hearts—but it will soon pass, although—jack of spades—a bad, dark young man will endeavor—seven of diamonds—to turn her into ridicule. The queen of clubs, being representative of herself, shows that it is towards her that the dark young man's malice will be directed. Now take the cards at either extremity of the line, and pair them together. The two first being the jack of hearts and the ten of diamonds, you may say: "A gay young bachelor is preparing to take a journey—ace of spades and queen of clubs—which will bring him to

Maria D'Andrea's Simple Spells With Playing Cards

the presence of the lady consulting the cards, and cause her great joy. Seven of diamonds and eight of hearts—scandal talked about a fair young girl. Ten of spades and ace of diamonds—tears shed upon receipt of a letter. Seven of spades and ten of hearts—great joy, mingled with slight sorrow. Seven of clubs and ace of clubs—a letter promising money. Jack of spades and king of spades—the winning of a lawsuit. The nine of hearts, being the one card left, promises complete success."

Now gather up the cards, shuffle, cut, and deal them out in five packs—one for the lady herself, one for the house, one for "those who do not expect it," one for "those who do expect it," and one for "the surprise," in the first deal, laying one card aside for "consolation." The rest are then equally distributed among the other five packs, which will four of them contain three cards, whilst the last only consists of two.

We will suppose the first packet for the lady herself to be composed of the ace of diamonds, the seven of clubs, and the ten of hearts. The interpretation would run thus:

"Ace of diamonds—a letter will be shortly received—seven of clubs—announcing the arrival of a small sum of money—ten of hearts—and containing some very joyful tidings."

The second pack, "for the house," containing the king of spades, the nine of hearts, and the jack of spades:

"The person consulting the cards will receive a visit—king of spades—from a lawyer—nine of hearts—which will greatly delight—jack of spades—a dark, ill-disposed young man."

The third pack, "for those who do not expect it," composed of the ace of spades, the jack of hearts, and the ace of clubs, would read:

"Ace of spades—pleasure in store for—jack of hearts—a gay young bachelor—ace of clubs—by means of money; but as the jack of hearts is placed between two aces, it is evident that he runs a great risk of being imprisoned; and from the two cards signifying respectively 'pleasure' and 'money,' that it will be for having run into debt." The fourth pack, "for those who do expect it," containing the eight of hearts, the queen of clubs, and the ten of diamonds:

"The eight of hearts—the love-affairs of a fair young girl will oblige—the queen of clubs—the person consulting the cards—ten of diamonds—to take a journey."

The fifth pack, "for the surprise," consists of the seven of spades and the ten of spades, meaning:

Maria D'Andrea's Simple Spells With Playing Cards

"Seven of spades—slight trouble—ten of spades—caused by some person's imprisonment—the card of consolation—seven of diamonds—which will turn out to have been a mere report."

THE FLORENCE MODE

A pack is taken of thirty-two selected cards, shuffled well and cut in three, then laid out in four rows of eight cards each. Significator is made any king or queen that may be preferred; then seven are counted from that significator from left to right, and from right to left, also crossways, always starting from the king or queen that represents the person consulting. The thoughts, which are supposed to be indicated by the jacks, may then be counted from, or the house, or a letter; in fact, anything about which information is desired; when this is explained, the cards are paired from each extremity, each pair being explained as arrived at till the pack is finished. They are now gathered up, shuffled and cut in three; then turned up by threes, the highest of each suit being taken out.

When three of equal value come together, such as three aces, three kings, etc., they must all be taken out; the same is to be done should three of a suit come together; this is to be repeated three times, shuffling and cutting between each, and when the pack has been gone through, any that are remaining over must be put on one side and not used. Seven cards are counted again from significator, and paired as before.

The meanings ascribed to some of the cards being different from those already given, are here stated:

Ten of Clubs—A journey or big building.

Eight of Clubs—Drink or vexation.

Ten of Spades—At night-time.

Nine of Spades—Disappointment or sickness.

Ten of Diamonds—Money.

Seven of Diamonds—Check or paper money; sometimes an article of jewelry.

Three Sevens—A loss.

Four Tens—A great social rise through powerful friends.

Two Jacks—Treachery.

Ten of Hearts—An entertainment.

Seven of Hearts—Delay or slight anxiety.

Maria D'Andrea's Simple Spells With Playing Cards

Seven of Spades—Speedily.

Seven of Diamonds and Ace of Spades—News read in the newspaper.

Ace of Spades and any Court Card—Photograph.

Two Red Tens with Ace of Diamonds—A wedding.

Two Black Tens with Ace of Spades—A funeral.

Eight and Nine of Clubs—Dinner or supper party.

Seven of Clubs—A present.

Three Eights—Good business transactions.

Three Nines—A removal.

Three Tens—A rise, either of money or social.

PAST, PRESENT AND FUTURE

The person wishing to try her fortune in this manner (we will suppose her to be a young, fair person, represented by the eight of hearts), must well shuffle, and cut with the left hand, the pack of thirty-two cards; after which she must lay aside the topmost and undermost cards, to form the surprise. There will now remain thirty cards, which must be dealt out in three parcels—one to the left, one in the middle, and one to the right.

The left-hand pack represents the Past; the middle, the Present; and the one on the right hand, the Future. She must commence with the Past, which we will suppose to contain these ten cards: The king of clubs, ace of spades, jack of diamonds, nine of diamonds, ace of hearts, jack of hearts, queen of hearts, king of spades, jack of clubs, and the king of hearts.

She would remark that picture-cards predominating was a favorable sign, also that the presence of three kings proves that powerful persons were interesting themselves in her affairs; the three jacks, however, are supposed to warn her to beware of false friends; the nine of diamonds, some great annoyance overcome by some good and amiable person, represented by the queen of hearts; the two aces, notice of a plot. Taking the cards in the order they lay: "The king of clubs—a frank, open hearted man—ace of spades—fond of gayety and pleasure, is disliked by—jack of diamonds—an unfaithful friend—nine of diamonds—who seeks to injure him. The ace of hearts—a love letter—jack of hearts—from a gay young bachelor to a fair amiable woman—queen of hearts—causes—king of spades—a lawyer to endeavor to injure the clever—jack of clubs—enterprising young man, who is saved from him by—the king of hearts—a good and powerful man. Nevertheless, as the jack of clubs is placed between two similar cards, he

Maria D'Andrea's Simple Spells With Playing Cards

has run great risk of being imprisoned through the machinations of his enemy."

The second parcel, the Present, containing the ten of diamonds, nine of spades, eight of spades, queen of diamonds, queen of clubs, eight of hearts, seven of spades, ten of spades, queen of spades, eight of diamonds, signifies:

"The ten of diamonds—a voyage or journey, at that moment taking place—nine of spades—caused by the death or dangerous illness of someone—eight of spades—whose state will occasion great grief—queen of diamonds—to a fair woman. The queen of clubs—an affectionate woman seeks to console—eight of hearts—a fair young girl, who is the person making the essay—seven of spades—who has secret griefs—ten of spades—causing her many tears—queen of spades—these are occasioned by the conduct of either a dark woman or a widow, who—eight of diamonds—is her rival."

The third packet of cards, the Future, we will suppose to contain the eight of clubs, ten of clubs, seven of diamonds, ten of hearts, seven of clubs, nine of hearts, ace of diamonds, jack of spades, seven of hearts, and the nine of clubs, which would read thus:

"In the first place, the large number of small cards foretells success in enterprises, although the presence of three sevens predicts an illness. The eight of clubs—a dark young girl—ten of clubs—is about to inherit a large fortune—seven of diamonds—but her satirical disposition will destroy—ten of hearts—all her happiness. Seven of clubs—a little money and—nine of hearts—much joy—ace of hearts—will be announced to the person making the essay by a letter, and—jack of spades—a wild young man—seven of hearts—will be overjoyed at receiving—nine of clubs—some unexpected tidings. The cards of surprise—viz., the king of diamonds and the ace of clubs—predict that a letter will be received from some military man and that it will contain money."

THE MATRIMONIAL ORACLE

In the case of consultation upon the subject of marriages in general, the Consultant should be withdrawn from the pack, inasmuch as it is necessary that the couple should be of the same color, in order that a marriage be formed.

Should the young lady be a blonde who consults the oracle upon questions of marriage, she should pick out the jack of hearts and the queen of hearts, and taking these two cards from out of the pack, place them aside; then, let her shuffle the cards well and again pick out eleven, which are in like manner set aside. Then take up the jack and queen of hearts and replace them among the remaining cards in the pack, shuffle them again, place them in succession in a line from right to left. It is necessary so that the marriage be an accomplished fact, that a quint, or five cards in hearts, appear in the lay-out, and, if it be found at the end of the deal

Maria D'Andrea's Simple Spells With Playing Cards

at your left, the marriage will be a certainty; but, should the nine of diamonds or the seven of spades be placed in front, the marriage will be most certainly delayed; should the nine of diamonds alone appear, the delay will be not over serious; but should, in place of these cards, there be found the king of spades inverted, or three tens, the marriage will never come off.

If the lady be a brunette she will take the jack of clubs, and, if very dark, the jack of spades as her representative husband, and represent herself by a queen of corresponding color, always taking care that the card ordinarily used as the Consultant be retired from the pack.

Should a widow desire to contract a second marriage, she represents herself as the queen of clubs and her future husband as the king of clubs, which cards should be retired and placed aside. Then the pack is shuffled well and dealt upon the table, face downward, in five rows; take these up again in a reversed manner, shuffle them well and cause the consultant to cut, and to select eleven from the pack, which are to be put aside. Then retake the king and queen of clubs, and place them among the remainder of the pack, whence the eleven have been withdrawn; shuffle well and again let them be cut, and then deal, placing the first one dealt upon the table directly in front of you in an isolated position—this is the surprise. Deal the others and place them in a single line below the surprise card on the table, ranging from right to left, one by one. Turn over all the cards except the surprise, which is only to be consulted after the rest. Read the cards thus placed likewise from right to left, and study their significations well. It is necessary, in order that the widow's desire for a second marriage be successful, that the queen of spades come out inverted, that the king of the same color likewise appear, and that the jack of spades be at the side of the ace of spades or of hearts, and under this combination her second marriage is an assured fact. Should the ace of spades emerge near the jack, it will also be necessary that the ace of hearts come out to effect an alliance; but, if the consultant have three tens before her, the marriage will not occur; and, should the nine of spades come out, it denotes absolute failure. Again, if instead of these cards the eight of clubs and the eight of hearts appear, the marriage will be a great success. Great care should be observed in noticing whether three eights appear behind the Consultant, for in that instance the marriage will not be a happy one.

THE STAR METHOD

We will suppose the person making the essay to be a widow, and consequently represented by the queen of spades. This card is, therefore, to be withdrawn from the pack, and laid face uppermost upon the table. The remaining thirty-one cards are then to be well shuffled, cut, the topmost card withdrawn and placed lengthwise, and face uppermost, above the head of the queen of spades. The cards

Maria D'Andrea's Simple Spells With Playing Cards

are to be shuffled, cut, and the topmost card withdrawn, twelve more times, the manner of their arrangement being this: The queen of spades in the center, the first card lengthwise above her head, the second ditto at her feet, the third on her right side, the fourth on her left, the fifth placed upright above the first, the sixth ditto below the second, the seventh at the right of the third, the eighth at the left of the fourth, the ninth, tenth, eleventh, and twelfth, at the four corners, and the thirteenth across the center card—the queen of spades—thus forming a star. (See engraving.) We will suppose the fourteenth card to be the queen of spades, which represents the person making the essay; then—1. Ace of hearts; 2. King of clubs; 3. Ten of clubs; 4. Nine of diamonds; 5. Queen of clubs; 6. Eight of hearts; 7. Ten of spades; 8. Jack of clubs; 9. Seven of clubs; 10. Ten of hearts; 11. Jack of diamonds; 12. Eight of diamonds; 13. Nine of clubs. These being placed at right angles, the person consulting them takes them up two by two, beginning with those last laid down.

The first card, 12, the eight of diamonds, and the one in the opposite corner, viz., 11, the jack of diamonds, read—"Overtures will be made—jack of diamonds—by a fair young man—next two cards, 10 and 9, ten of hearts—which will prove unsuccessful—seven of clubs—on account of something connected with money. Next two cards, 8 and 7, the jack of clubs—a clever dark young man—ten of spades—will be greatly grieved by, 6—eight of hearts, a fair girl to whom he is attached. Next two cards, 5 and 4, the queen of clubs—a dark woman—nine of diamonds—will be annoyed at not receiving, 3—ten of clubs—a sum of money—next two cards, 2 and 1, the king of clubs—which was to have been sent her by a generous dark man, who is fond of obliging his friends—ace of hearts—it will at last arrive, accompanied by a love-letter—13th card, placed across the queen of spades, nine of clubs—and be the cause of unexpected gain to the person consulting the cards."

SHORTER STAR METHOD

The shorter and simpler star method surrounds the card representing the person trying his or her fortune with a less number of cards. The cards are shuffled and cut as before described, and the topmost one withdrawn. We will suppose the center card to be the jack of clubs, representing a dark young man. The first topmost one proves to be the ace of clubs and is placed above the head of the jack. The second, the eight of hearts, is placed at his feet; the third, the jack of diamonds, at his right; the fourth, the queen of spades, at his left. These are now read: Ace of clubs—"you will soon receive a letter which will give you great pleasure"—eight of hearts—"from a fair girl"—jack of diamonds—"a man in uniform"—queen of spades—"and a malicious widow will seek to injure you on that very account."

Maria D'Andrea's Simple Spells With Playing Cards

WISHES

Having finished all the different methods of laying the cards, various indications will now be given which are supposed to show whether the one who is consulting will obtain his or her wish. These are done in various methods, and each is given in order.

WISH NO. I.

The pack of thirty-two selected cards having been well shuffled and cut, proceed by turning them up by threes; if an ace appears amongst the three, those three cards must be taken out; and if the nine of hearts and the significator appear, they must also be taken out with the cards that accompany them. This operation has to be repeated three times, and if in the three times the four aces, the significator and the nine of hearts come out in eleven or nine cards, then the wish is taken to be certain; if they do not appear under twelve or fifteen, it is said the wish will not come to pass. To make the meaning perfectly clear, we will suppose that a dark man, represented by the king of clubs, is making the essay. Having well shuffled and cut the cards, they must be turned up in threes.

In the first come the king of diamonds, ace of spades, and king of clubs—the person who is making the essay; the next three are king and queen of spades and ten of diamonds—these are useless; the next three, the ten of hearts, six of diamonds and king of hearts—these are laid on one side; then the seven and eight of spades and ace of diamonds—these are withdrawn and are put over the other three, with the ace and significator; the next three—nine of diamonds, eight of clubs and ace of clubs, these come out; likewise the jack of clubs, ten of spades, and ace of hearts, and the two left are the jack of spades and nine of hearts—the other cards are useless. Fourteen cards are now left, they are shuffled and cut, and again dealt in threes.

The ace of spades, nine of hearts, king of spades remain; the next three, ten of spades, ace of hearts and nine of diamonds also remain. The following triplet: king of diamonds, king of clubs and jack of clubs all come out. The seven of spades, ace of diamonds and eight of clubs remain, as also the two last—eight of spades and ace of clubs. This makes eleven cards, so that the wish is considered to be gained; but if it is tried the third time, and more cards come out, then it is supposed that it will be very speedily accomplished.

WISH NO. II.

Shuffle and cut the pack of thirty-two selected cards. Put them together, and turn up in threes. Supposing there should be two of one suit, and one of another, the highest is taken out. Should there be three of one suit, all are to be withdrawn and laid on the table in front of the dealer, in the shape of a semi-circle or horse

Maria D'Andrea's Simple Spells With Playing Cards

shoe. If three of equal value, such as three kings, or three tens, they are likewise to come out. The pack is gone through, then shuffled and cut again. When the end of the pack is arrived at, this is repeated a third time, acting in the same manner. Now count from the significator, or if that should not appear naturally, use the jack (which is taken to represent the thoughts of the person consulting); seven are counted each way till it is come back to, then the cards are paired from end to end, being read as arrived at; then all the cards are shuffled together, cut in three, and dealt out in packets of four, face downward. Each packet is taken up and looked through, the cards being turned up one by one till an ace is come to. Should there be no ace in the parcel it is put on one side—it is useless. The cards are shuffled and cut again, being turned up as before, and dealt in three packets, stopping each time at the ace, as before. The third time they are shuffled but *not* cut, and dealt in packets of two, and proceeded with as before. Should the four aces (in the last deal) turn up without another card, the wish is supposed to be sure, and to come at once. If they come out with hearts, or diamonds, there will be some delay, but if the nine or seven of spades makes its appearance with the aces, then it is said to be a sign of disappointment.

WISH NO. III.

A pack is taken of thirty-two selected cards, and cut with the left hand; thirteen cards are then dealt out. If amongst these is to be found one or more aces, lay them aside. The remaining ones are shuffled and cut and thirteen again dealt; the aces are withdrawn as before, and again shuffled, cut and dealt. If in these three deals all four aces make their appearance, it is supposed that the wish will be granted. If all the aces come at the first deal, the answer is taken to be in the highest degree favorable. If in the three times only one or two appear, it is considered that the wish will not be granted.

WISH NO. IV.

A pack of thirty-two selected cards is shuffled and cut, the consultant wishing all the time. They are laid out in two rows of four each, face downwards. When two pairs come up, they must be covered by the cards held in the dealer's hand. Should it be possible to cover each pair—such as two kings, two queens, etc., it is supposed that the wish will be granted. If the cards do not pair easily, it is said the wish will not come to pass, or, at any rate, not for a long period.

The following is taken to show whether the wish will be granted: The cards are well shuffled, the consultant keeping his thoughts all the time fixed upon whatever wish he may have formed; the cards are cut once, and the card cut is noted; they are shuffled again and dealt out into three parcels—each of these being examined in turn, and if it is found that the card turned up next, either the one representing the dealer or the person who is consulting him—the ace of hearts or the

Maria D'Andrea's Simple Spells With Playing Cards

nine of hearts, it is said that the wish will be granted. If it be in the same parcel with any of these, without being next to them, it is supposed there is a chance of the wish coming to pass at some more distant period; but if the nine of spades makes its appearance, it is taken that a disappointment is possible.

WISH NO. V.

The pack of thirty-two selected cards, as in the foregoing method, is taken, shuffled and cut; then the four aces are taken out, the significator, or the person for whom the dealer is acting, and anything he wants to know about—such as money, then the ten of diamonds would be selected; if about a man, any king; if about a woman, any queen; if about business, the ten of clubs. These are shuffled after having been withdrawn, without cutting, and the nine of spades, which is the disappointment card, is also added to the aces, etc., in all seven cards, laying them face downwards on the table. Then the remainder are taken, shuffled well, and turned up in threes twice, the one following being the seventh. The pack is gone through like this, and when the nine of hearts appears whatever number that falls on in the twenty-five cards remaining. When one, two, three, four, five, six or seven, it must fall on the card drawn out by the seven cards abstracted thus; if it should fall on No. 1 and that happens on an ace, it is favorable, and if he should chance on an ace, or his wish, or anything but the disappointment card (nine of spades), the wish will be realized.

First of all, the four aces are taken out, and the nine of spades, (the disappointment card); then, supposing the dealer is acting for a fair man, or a soldier, who is anxious to know whether he will get his wish. We will imagine he has invested a sum of money, and he wishes to know whether it is a good one; or that he hopes for a legacy and is anxious to know if he will get it. The king of diamonds (representing the fair man), and the ten of diamonds, the money card, should therefore be taken out. These are added to the four aces and the nine of spades. These are well shuffled, but not cut, and laid face downwards on the table, like the following:

These represent the four aces, the disappointment card and the inquirer and his wish. The remaining cards are now taken and turned up three at a time. We will suppose the first three are the nine, seven and eight of clubs; the next three the ten and jack of hearts, and eight of diamonds; and the seventh card, the queen of clubs—these are passed by. Begin again, counting one. We will suppose the next three are the eight of spades, the seven of clubs and the nine of hearts. Three are then counted from those laid face downwards on the table, and that card is turned up—we will suppose that to be the king of diamonds; the cards turned up by threes are gathered together and shuffled, and turned up by sevens

Maria D'Andrea's Simple Spells With Playing Cards

as before. Should the nine of hearts fall on the fourth card the second time, that is to be turned up—we will suppose that to be the ace of diamonds. Proceed again as before, and this time we will imagine the nine of hearts to fall on the seventh—this may be the ten of diamonds—so that it could be said to the persons consulting that it is said he will get his wish; but supposing the nine of hearts to fall on the fifth card, and that turns out to be the nine of spades, he will be disappointed; and should it happen that *in the first reading* the nine of hearts should come on, we will say, the first card, which might prove the nine of spades, then it is no use continuing the three times, as it is supposed there is no chance whatever of the wish being realized.

WISH NO. VI.

The whole pack of fifty-two cards is taken, shuffled and cut in two packets. They are now laid out face uppermost, in three rows of four cards each, in all twelve cards. If in the first twelve cards any court cards appear, they are taken out, filling up the spaces with fresh cards; should these again be court cards, they are abstracted as before, filling in the spaces as described; if not, they are thus counted: Eleven must be made up of any *two* cards, such as an ace and ten (ace counting as one), and covered, or two and nine, each card being covered as counted, three and eight, four and seven, five and six, etc. If a court card appears, it is a stop and counts as nothing. If, as the cards are covered, eleven can be made out of any of the two cards, and continued to the end, exhausting all the cards, it is taken that the wish will be gained; in that case all the court cards ought to be on the top, as those cast aside at first are used at the last, to cover each two cards as they count eleven. If the court cards cannot be got to come out at the end, the wish is supposed to be delayed, and if eleven cannot be made from nearly the beginning, it is said, the wish will not be realized at all. To explain the meaning more clearly, the following diagram is given. We will suppose they are as follows:—

There are now removed the three court cards, viz.:—the jack of clubs in the first row, the jack of diamonds in the second, and the king of diamonds in the third. These are replaced by the nine of clubs in the first row, five of spades in the second, and six of hearts in the third. The cards are now to be covered. In the first row, four and seven of spades, making respectively eleven covered by ten of clubs and ten of spades. Eleven is now made, where possible, from all three rows. In the second row will be found the six and five of spades; these are covered by two and one of clubs. In the third row, one of clubs and ten of hearts, covered by seven of diamonds and three of spades. In the same row, five of diamonds and six of hearts, covered by the two of diamonds and king of hearts. In the first and second rows, nine of clubs and two of spades, covered by the four and eight of diamonds. In the second row, three and eight of diamonds, covered by the jack of hearts and queen of clubs. In the first and second row, the one and ten of spades, covered by the three of hearts and three of spades. In the first and third rows, four of clubs and seven of diamonds, covered by the ten of diamonds and nine of hearts. In the third row, nine of hearts and two of diamonds, covered by the five of clubs and ace of diamonds. In the first and third rows, ten of clubs and ace of diamonds, covered by the seven of hearts and queen of diamonds. In the first row, four of diamonds and seven of hearts, covered by the eight and five of hearts. In the first and third rows, eight of hearts and three of clubs, covered by the seven of clubs and jack of spades. In the first and second rows, seven of clubs and four of hearts, covered by the two of clubs and eight of spades. In the first and second rows, the three of hearts and eight of spades, covered by the king and nine of spades. In the first row, two of clubs and nine of spades, covered by the ace of hearts and six of diamonds. In the first row, again, the ace of hearts and ten of diamonds, covered by the two of hearts and six of clubs. In the first and third rows, five and six of clubs, covered by the nine of diamonds and queen of hearts. In the first row, five of hearts and six of diamonds, covered by the king and eight of clubs. Then in the first and second rows, the eight of clubs and three of spades, as there is only one card remaining, viz.:—the queen of spades, the three other cards to be covered, those put aside at first are taken up, the last two to be covered being the nine of diamonds and two of hearts, covered by the jack of diamonds and jack of clubs. In this case the wish is supposed to be realized; but in some cases it will be found that it has not made up the number eleven in the two cards, and then it is taken that the wish may be either delayed or not fulfilled.

Maria D'Andrea's Simple Spells With Playing Cards

CURIOUS GAMES WITH CARDS

By Which Fortunes Are Told in a Most Singular and Diverting Manner.

LOVERS' HEARTS.

Four young persons, but not more, may play at this game, or three by making a dummy hand. This game is played exactly the same in every game, making the queen, which is called Venus, above the ace; the ace in this game only stands for one, and hearts must be led off by the person next the dealer. He or she who gets most tricks this way (each taking up their own and no partnership) is supposed to have most lovers, and the king and queen of hearts in one hand is said to denote matrimony at hand; but woe to the unlucky one who gets no tricks at the deal, or does not hold a heart in his or her hand; to them are ascribed misfortune in love and long tarry before they marry.

LOVE'S LOTTERY.

Let each one present deposit any sum agreed on, or a certain number of counters; put a complete pack of cards well shuffled in a bag, let the parties stand in a circle and the bag being handed round, each draw three; pairs of any kind are supposed to be favorable omens of some good fortune about to occur to the party and get back from the pool the sum that each agreed to pay. The king of hearts is here made the god of love, and claims double, and professes to give a faithful swain to the fair one who has the good fortune to draw him; if Venus, the queen of hearts, is with him, it is the conquering prize, and clears the pool; fives and nines are reckoned crosses and misfortunes, and pay a forfeit of the sum agreed on to the pool, besides the usual stipend at each new game; three nines at one draw is supposed to portend the lady will be an old maid, three fives, a bad husband.

MATRIMONY.

Let three, five, or seven young women stand in a circle, and draw a card out of a bag. It is taken that she who gets the highest card will be the first married of the company, whether she be at the present time maid, wife, or widow, and she

Maria D'Andrea's Simple Spells With Playing Cards

who has the lowest has the longest time to stay ere the sun shines on her wedding day; she who draws the ace of spades will never bear the name of wife; and she who has the nine of hearts in this trial will have one lover too many to her sorrow.

CUPID'S PASTIME.

Amusement may be caused by this game to all those playing, and at the same time it is supposed that some curious particulars may be learned concerning the future fates of the consultants.

Several may play at the game, it requiring no special number, only leaving out nine cards on the table not exposed to view; each person puts a trifling sum in the pool, and the dealer double. The ace of diamonds is made principal, and takes all the other aces, etc.; twos and threes in hand are said to show luck; fours, a continuance in the present state; fives, trouble; sixes, profit; sevens, worries; eights, disappointment; nines, surprises; tens, settlements; jacks, sweethearts; kings and queens, friends and acquaintances; ace of spades, death; ace of clubs, a letter; and the ace of diamonds with ten of hearts, marriage.

The ace of diamonds being played first, or should it be amongst the nine, the dealer calls for the queen of hearts, which takes next. If the ace be not out and the queen conquers, it is supposed that the person who played her will be married that year without a doubt, though it may perhaps seem unlikely at that time; but if she loses her queen, she must wait longer. The ace and queen being called, the rest go in rotation as at whist; kings taking queens, queens jacks, and so on, and the more tricks taken, the more money the winner gets off the board on the division; those who hold the nine of spades are to pay a penny to the board, and it is said they will have some trouble; but the fortunate fair one who holds the queen and jack of hearts in the same hand is supposed soon to be married, or if she is already within the pale of matrimony, a great rise in life by means of her husband; those who hold the ace of diamonds and queen of hearts clear the money off the board and end that game; it also professes to betoken great prosperity.

WEDDING BELLS.

You select the four kings from a pack, and lay them side by side in a row upon the table.

The lady who wishes to know her fortune gives to each of these cards the name of some gentleman of her acquaintance who might be likely to woo her in marriage. It is usual to pronounce these names aloud before the company. The name given to the king of hearts is, however, an exception. This secret the lady keeps to herself. To these four kings, you can also add a queen, which then denotes the old maid.

Maria D'Andrea's Simple Spells With Playing Cards

Now, take the rest of the pack, shuffle it thoroughly, let the person in question cut three times and commence. Under each of the above-named picture-cards you lay a card in turn, and as often as a spade is placed under a spade, a heart under a heart, *et cetera*, that is, as often as a card of the same suit is placed under one of these picture-cards, the picture-card is turned from its position.

The first time it takes a direction from left to right, the second time it lies upside down, the third time it is raised again to a position from right to left, and the fourth and last time it regains its former upright position.

That one of the four kings who, after these different changes, first resumes his upright position, is to be the happy husband. If it should happen to be the old maid, you can imagine what is in store for you.

MARRIAGE QUESTIONS.

After having learned from the cards who is to be the husband, the questions next asked are, usually: How much will he love his wife, why he marries her, and what is his profession. These questions are answered in the following manner:

Gather up the cards, shuffle them thoroughly, and let the person cut them three times. Then tell off the cards upon the table, as you recite the following sentence:

Heartily, painfully,Beyond all measure.By fits and starts.Not a bit in the world.

You repeat this sentence until the king of hearts makes his appearance. If it happens that, as you lay this upon the table, you pronounce the word "heartily" he will love his future wife heartily, and so on.

Now as to why he marries her. Count off the cards upon the table, while you repeat the following sentence:

For love, for her beauty,For his parents' command,For the bright, golden dollars,For counsel of friends.

The sentence by which you discover what is his profession is the following:

Gentleman, alderman, clergyman, doctor,Merchant, broker, professor, major,Mechanic, lawyer, shipmaster, tailor.

This method of telling fortunes is very entertaining in society, when you have not the book to find more particular answers.

Maria D'Andrea's Simple Spells With Playing Cards

WHO IS MARIA D' ANDREA?

Maria D' Andrea is an internationally-known, professional psychic born in Hungary. She is a published author, shaman, healing minister and officiates at ceremonies as well as working as a parapsychologist, speaker/lecturer and hosting her own weekly TV show.

Maria has demonstrated psychic ability since she was a child and has been sharing her abilities and helping others make better decisions on their Path of Life for over forty years. Maria specializes in rune casting. However, she is fluent in all metaphysical, psychic and spiritual disciplines and has the ability to adjust her readings to an individual's preference. She is well known as a spiritual leader and for teaching all aspects of the spiritual/PSI/occult fields.

Some of her other abilities include serving as a trance medium, reading the tarot, past lives, home cleansing, dowsing, numerology, clairvoyance, business consulting and E Mei Qu Gong.

She has been a popular radio and television guest and is the hostess of her own Cablevision TV Series "The Spiritual World With Maria." Maria is also the founder of several organizations such as The D'Andrea Institute of Esoteric Studies.

WEBSITE: www.MariaDAndrea.com

PUBLISHED WORKS
Maria's books are published by Timothy Beckley's Inner Light Publications and are available from Amazon.com

How To Eliminate Stress And Anxiety Through The Occult

Heaven Sent Money Spells

Maria D' Andrea's Secret Occult Gallery And Spell Casting Formulary

Your Personal Mega Power Spells

Occult Grimoire And Magical Formulary

Secret Magical Elixirs Of Life

SPELLCRAFT, WISECRAFT, OCCULT, METAPHYSICS
Workbooks And Study Guides From Qualified Instructors

MARIA D' ANDREA

Maria is a gifted psychic, spiritual counselor, and shaman. She has helped those in matters of luck, love and financial concerns. She lectures, holds workshops and does private counseling in NY area. Her books are exclusively published by Tim Beckley.

HEAVEN SENT MONEY SPELLS
IMAGINE RECEIVING MONEY JUST BY USING THE POWERS OF YOUR MIND! Let Maria D' Andrea Tell You How To Turn Your Dreams Into Cash — And Become A Virtual Human MONEY MAGNET. Inspired by the Heavenly Light. Here are spells that anyone can learn to execute. Use herbs, candles and gemstones to create prosperity! Have talismans and amulets help do the work for you!
8.5x11—Workbook format—132 pages—ISBN-13: 978-1606111000—$19.95

SECRET OCCULT GALLERY AND SPELL CASTING FORMULARY
COME UP TO THE "GOOD LIFE" with Maria's top dozen enchantments and occult gallery of mystical and spiritual essentials. Easy to perform spells that could put you on easy street.
8.5x11—Workbook format—152 pages—ISBN-13: 978-1606111284—$21.95

YOUR PERSONAL MEGA POWER SPELLS
A valuable interpretation of blessings, protections, hex-breaking rituals and ceremonies as practiced by the most ardent of Wiccans, alchemists, sages and occultists down through the centuries.
8.5X11—252 pages—ISBN-13: 978-1606111055—$21.95

SECRET MAGICAL ELIXIRS OF LIFE
Explore The Paranormal Vibrations Of Crystals, Gems And Stones For Good Health, Enhanced Psychic Powers And Phenomenal Inner Strength!
8.5X11—150 PAGES—ISBN-13: 978-1606111147—$21.95

HOW TO ELIMINATE ANXIETY AND STRESS THROUGH THE OCCULT
Just utilize Crystals, Gemstones, Meditation, Herbs, Oils, Visualization, Chakras, Music, Prayer, Mandalas, Mantras, Incense, Candles and More.
6x9—150 pages—ISBN-13: 978-1606111383—$19.95

MYSTICAL, MAGICKAL BEASTS AND BEINGS
Come explore the supernatural side of man's best – and worst – "friends" as related in the strangest stories involving beasties of all sorts – seen and unseen. And uppermost learn how to get them to assist in our lives in a positive way. Other contributors include Penny Melis and Sean Casteel.
8.5x11—224 pages—ISBN-13: 978-1606111567—$21.95

OCCULT GRIMORIE AND MAGICAL FORMULARY
10 BOOKS ROLLED INTO ONE! – OVER 500 SPELLS! Reveals the secret of the ages. Manifest your destiny NOW! Most powerful spellcasters deliberately leave out important information. NOT MARIA!
8.5x11—236 pages—ISBN-13: 978-1606111086—$24.00

SUPER SPECIAL: Retail customers get all of Maria's books as listed for $139.00 + $15.00 Postage/Shipping. FREE DVD WITH 3 OF MARIA'S BOOKS OR MORE

HERE ARE THE LATEST MYSTICAL SECRETS FROM FAMED HUNGARIAN BORN PSYCHIC MARIA D'ANDREA, REVEALED IN HER NEW BOOK AND VIDEO DRAMATIZATION

COME UP TO THE "GOOD LIFE" WITH MARIA'S TOP ONE DOZEN SPELLS AND OCCULT GALLERY OF MYSTICAL AND SPIRITUAL ESSENTIALS

$24.00 + $5 S/H

Though most popularly known as the "Money Psychic," Hungarian born Maria D' Andrea is actually knowledgeable on a wide range of paranormal topics. Each week she focuses on a different topic in her widely seen TV show <u>The Spritiual World With Maria</u> broadcast throughout Long Island. In addition, she has given lectures and seminars on subjects that are widely diverse.

In her latest work (accompanied by a Free Bonus DVD), <u>**MARIA D' ANDREA'S SECRET OCCULT GALLERY AND SPELL CASTING FORMULARY,**</u> she delves into over fifty little known aspects of the occult. In addition, scattered amongst the pages are twelve of her most powerful spells that she has only shared up until now with her most privileged students.

WHY THIS OCCULT GALLERY IS IMPORTANT TO YOU— TOPICS DISCUSSED

Psychic Self-Defense · How Herbs Relate To Spiritual Work · Energy Streams: Mother Nature's Party Lines · Are You A Modern Day Prophet? Children In The Path Of Light · Manifesting Your Own Future · Utilizing The Power Of Belief · Communicating On A Psychic Level How To Be Guided By Spiritual Realms · The Secret Power Within Crystals And Candles · Journey To Another Plane Earth Changes And How They Affect You · Stones of Intrigue · Living An Alpha Reality · UFOs And Crystals Colored Lights - Effects of Being Exposed To Them · How To Use "Wind Magic" · Choices On Your Path · U.F.O.'s On The Astral Plane Identifing Forms With Power · Lucid Dreams · Ghosts Versus Spirits · Sounds Of Power · Symbolic Magick And Its Many Uses My Invisible Partners · Imagination Versus Psychic: How To Identify · Prosperity And Happiness All Yours! When To Tell You Are Guided By Spirit Beings · Out Of Body Travel Without Baggage · Telepathy: Direct Communication Ghostology: Finding Unseen Forces · The Inner Kingdom · New Age Formulary · Hobgoblins · Ghost Of The Tribes · The Tidra The Link Between Realities · Story Of The Bats · Empowerment Through The Word Influence Of UFOs On Spiritual Awareness · Dreams: Your Direct Phone Line · Dream Pillows · God's Creatures - Our Psychic Connection Psychic Rune Casting to Native Indian Crafts · Universal Lines Of Force · Tree Doctor

Revealed: Maria's Most Powerful Spells Never Published Previously! Easy To Follow And Perform Yourself

SPELL 1 – LOVE AND GOD
SPELL 2 – MANIFEST WITH THE GOD BOX
SPELL 3 — KEEPS NEGATIVITY AWAY
SPELL 4 – SEA MAGIC FOR ANY WISH
SPELL 5 – TO RELEASE ANGER
SPELL 6 – HELP FOR AN ANGELIC SPIRIT
SPELL 7 – SPELLS WITH GODDESS FREYJA
SPELL 8 – TO BRING IN LUCK
SPELL 9 – THE SPELL OF LOVE
SPELL 10 - THE WHIM OF THE GODS SPELL
SPELL 11   SUCCESS SPELL OF THE DRAGON KINGS
SPELL 12 – HAPPINESS AND HARMONY SPELL

HOW TO ORDER – This remarkable book and study guide with its bonus DVD is bound to enhance your being. If you are looking for success this progressive metaphysical volume is for you. And if you want a great Occult Gallery filled with a wondrous trove of information and facts, send just $24.00 + $5 S/H and request **MARIA'S OCCULT GALLERY**. It will be a decision you will be happy to have made.

SUPER SPECIAL
5 BOOKS AND 5 DVDS IN AD $99.00 + $10 S/H

TIMOTHY G. BECKLEY · BOX 753
NEW BRUNSWICK, NJ 08903

OTHER BENEFICIAL TITLES BY MARIA D' ANDREA

EACH BOOK COMES WITH A FREE DVD
All books are large format Study Guides

( ) <u>**HEAVEN SENT MONEY SPELLS**</u>
Learn why Maria is known as the "Money Psychc" as she brings prosperity into your life with these easy to do spells. - **$21.95**

( ) <u>**YOUR PERSONAL MEGA POWER SPELLS**</u>
Hundreds of love spells, money spells, spells for protection against negative forces. Enhance your entire being. -- **$25.00**

( ) <u>**OCCULT GRIMOIRE AND MAGICAL FORMULARY**</u>
500 spells to manifest your own future destiny. Benefits of using candles, crystals, herbs. All positive information. - **$25.00**

( ) <u>**SECRET MAGICKAL ELIXIRS OF LIFE**</u>
Turn a glass of water into a powerful elixir for improved good health, enhanced psychic abilities and the fortification of inner strength. - **$25.00**

ALSO AVAILABLE
SPECIALLY PREPARED GEMSTONE KIT
YOU CAN USE WITH MARIA'S BOOKS & DVDS

Contains green agate, amethyst, carnelian, citrine, hematite, green jasper, rose quartz, green quartz, clear quartz, sodalite, and tiger's eye, and a vial of lavender oil and a blue travel bag.

ADD THIS KIT TO YOUR ORDER FOR JUST $20.00

WILLAM ALEXANDER ORIBELLO

At an early age, Oribello encountered Angelic Beings. Later in life he was taught by the Masters of Wisdom a variety of occult secrets which he has used to guide many. His teachings combine the Christian Mysteries with the art of Spiritism.

THE MASTERBOOK OF SPIRITUAL POWER—The spells in this sacred text work like a magnet to attract big money, good health, love, freedom from tension and worry...as well as banishing curses and eroding negativity.

8.5x11—116 pages—ISBN-13: 978-1606111109—$18.95

THE SEALED MAGICAL BOOK OF MOSES—Here are arcane secrets of Moses' powers that can now be revealed to series students only. Includes the 21 MAGICAL TALISMANS OF MOSES seldom seen, which can give you the powers of the holy sage.

8.5x11—142 pages—ISBN-13: 978-0938294689—$18.95

CANDLE BURNING MAGIC WITH THE PSALMS—Create life's greatest blessings by combining the power of the Holy Psalms with the magic of burning different colored candles. Best times, days and conditions for spells.

8.5x11—188 pages—ISBN-13: 978-0938294580—$21.95

USING CANDLE BURNING TO CONTACT YOUR GUARDIAN ANGEL

8.5X11—100 pages—ISBN-13: 978-0938294757—$19.95

SACRED MAGIC REVISED—Forbidden knowledge now revealed...prosperity for all guaranteed! Includes seven great money secrets.

8.5x11—146 pages—ISBN-13: 978-1606111291—$18.95

DIVINE BIBLE SPELLS—This book proves what you've heard all along – With God All Things Are Possible! Added material from Dragonstar.

8.5x11—142 pages—ISBN-13: 978-1606111499—$18.95

DIVINE MONEY SPELLS—Easy Magickal Spells To Jump Start Your Spiritual Economic Stimulus Package Added material from Dragonstar. Spells to eliminate poverty and to draw abundance.

8.5x11—152 pages—ISBN-13: 978-1606110645—$21.95

THE MEDIUMSHIP OF SPIRIT—The Ascension of William Alexander Oribello. Now an Ascended Master, Oribello has returned to the Earth Plane to continue his great work, assisted by the mediumship of psychic Aurora Thyme...

8.5X11—122 pages—ISBN-13: 978-1606111512—$18.95

GODSPELLS: WRITTEN SPELLS, SPOKEN SPELLS AND SPELL ENHANCERS—Here are the rules laid down thousands of years ago by those who spoke with the Heavenly Host and learned of his TRUE wishes for all of mankind. NOT of the devil. For unselfish use only!

8.5x11—140 pages—ISBN-13: 978-0938294498—$18.95

COUNT SAINT GERMAIN - THE MAN WHO LIVES FOREVER—Let Count Saint Germain — the man who lives forever — help transform your life through his insight into the metaphysical laws that govern the universe. "Strange" bio by Art Crocket. Channelings of the Master by Wm Oribello.

8.5x11—132 pages—ISBN-13: 978-1892062208—$21.95

Add $20 for DVD of Oribello channeling Saint Germain under the purple ray.

CURSES AND THEIR REVERSALS— Plus: Omens, Superstitions And The Removal Of The Evil Eye. Important workbook by Oribello with Maria D' Andrea, Lady Suzanne and others.

8.5x11—182 pages—ISBN-13: 978-1606111406—$21.95

SUPER SPECIAL
Mail Order customers get all of Wm Oribello's books as listed for just $149.95 + $15.00 SH

Mail Order Customers – Book Stores – Wholesalers – Distributors
Order Directly From
TIMOTHY G BECKLEY, BOX 753, NEW BRUNSWICK, NJ 08903
mrufo8@hotmail.com   credit card orders   732 602-3407

WILLIAM ALEXANDER ORIBELLO

REVISED AND UPDATED – "DOUBLE IN SIZE" – EDITIONS

WITH DOZENS OF NEW SPELLS AND SPIRITUAL ADVICE! EVEN TALISMANS YOU CAN COPY AND USE TO IMPROVE YOUR LIFE!

**FORBIDDEN KNOWLEDGE NOW REVEALED
PROSPERITY FOR ALL GUARANTEED!
$20 each – All 3 For Just $54.95**

( ) Sacred Magic Revised_ _ _

**Discover Occult Secrets That Are Thousands Of Years Old!
INCLUDES SEVEN GREAT MONEY SECRETS!**

Here is forbidden knowledge that was originally applied to Moses, the Three Wise Men and Jesus.

As we approach the threshold of a Golden Age fill with chaos and confusion, humankind finds itself searching for practical answers to life's many problems.

The author - who has been a notable researcher and teacher in Spiritual Science for nearly three decades - offers well-tested techniques that can be applied by anyone wishing to improve his or her life. In the pages of this magical book, you will learn how to release the awesome power of your inner self to:

* Be prosperous, regardless of conditions around you by applying the SEVEN GREAT MONEY SECRETS.
* Develop your Psychic Powers in a safe and powerful manner by UNLOCKING THE SECRETS OF NATURE.
* Know and apply the hidden secrets to be found within COLORS, STONES and CANDLES, as well as the POWER OF THE SPOKEN WORD.
* Discover the secret clues from nature that will reveal your future concerning love, money, and how to maximize your chances for good luck and success.

You will also learn how to use a magic mirror to look into the future as well as how to find your individual lucky numbers to win at games of chance and bring you all that you deserve and desire.

The principles taught in this revised edition of a most popular work are NOT of the devil, but are based entirely upon God's word as handed down by the true Masters of all time.

( ) Godspells: Written Spells, Spoken Spells and Spell Enhancers

NOT OF THE DEVIL! EVERY SPELL IS OF THE LORD! TAKE MATTERS INTO YOUR OWN HANDS TO HAVE A MORE POSITIVE LIFE!

Here are the rules laid down thousands of years ago by those who spoke with the Heavenly Host and learned of his TRUE wishes for all of mankind.

Between the lines of sacred scriptures such as the Holy Bible we find many cryptic messages to establish this fact. Even the word Gospel is taken from ancient words meaning God Spell, and with that thought the author gives you the gift of wisdom in this book.

Here are fast working spells for many occasions: * Spells to overcome wickedness. * Good fortune spells. * Psychic development spell. * Business and money drawing spell. * Love and youthfulness.

Included are rare and powerful legendary power squares which have been handed down for centuries only in sacred volumes used by a select few. If you want to take matters into your own hands and live by the Golden Rule. This is a work you will cherish and work from for a long time. And do not feel ashamed to tell your friends who are not afraid to go beyond what the church teaches to purchase a copy of this title for themselves.

OVER 90 TITLES AVAILABLE ON KINDLE. KINDLE BOOKS CAN BE DOWNLOADED FROM ANY PC.

( ) The Sealed Magical Book Of Moses

This is valuable information to have on hand and give you an insight as to the depth of what the organized religions won't reveal. The power that Moses had, the ability to command things to happen wasn't just a one way street, it was a two-way communication and his Egyptian knowledge of magick was transferred to the monotheistic belief system he helped to set up.

Here are secrets of Moses' powers that can now be revealed for the serious student of the New Age and Occult. Included are the 21 MAGICAL TALISMANS OF MOSES seldom seen, which can be used to: * Bring the reader the highest possible good fortunes. * Attain honor and personal wealth. * Bring back a loved one or straying mate. * Help overcome illness and stay healthy.

This book contains ancient spells, charms and powerful commands given to Moses by God to help the Chosen People overcome all obstacles and vanquish their enemies. Now 142 pages!

SPECIAL MOSES KIT WITH SPECIAL TALISMAN – If you would like this kit designed by Wm Oribello add $25 to your order.

Want to Know More? Add these privately shot DVDs to your order (not filmed in Hollywood!)

( ) **GET RICH QUICK MONEY SPELLS**

( ) **SECRET SIGNS AND SYMBOLS TO CONTACT COUNT SAINT GERMAIN AND OTHER ASCENDED MASTERS**

( ) **5 EASY STEPS TO PSYCHIC SELF DEFENSE**
Approx 80 minutes each. $21.95 each

All Oribello items in this ad (3 books, 3 DVDs, Moses Kit)
just $135.00 + $10 S/H

Order From: Timothy G. Beckley, Box 753, New Brunswick, NJ 08903
PayPal Orders To: mrufo8@hotmail.com   732 602-3407 (order hot line)

THIS WILL BLOW YOUR MIND!

IS A "BREAKAWAY CIVILIZATION"
RESPONSIBLE FOR A SECRET "INVISIBLE" SPACE PROGRAM?

DID THE NAZIS LAND ON THE MOON AND MARS
DURING THE FINAL DAYS OF WORLD WAR II?

HAVE ASTRONAUTS PLANTED THE MASONIC FLAG
ON BOTH INTERPLANETARY BODIES?

WAS THE SUPER SCIENTIST NIKOLA TESLA INVOLVED IN THE
EARLY DEVELOPMENT OF THIS SECRET SPACE PROGRAM?

HAVE SCIENTISTS AND OTHERS BEEN TRAVELING BACK AND FORTH
BETWEEN SPACE COLONIES FOR DECADES?

228 PAGE MANUAL AND BONUS DVD!

An all time best seller just $20 with SUPER SPECIAL "The Eagle Has Landed" Bonus DVD.
Ask for THE SECRET SPACE PROGRAM

TESLA? THE NAZIS? NASA? OR AN UNKNOWN GROUP THAT REMAINS "INVISIBLE" TO OUR SENSES?

TIMOTHY G. BECKLEY, BOX 753, NEW BRUNSWICK, NJ 08903

OVER 90 TITLES AVAILABLE ON KINDLE AND NOOK. BOOKS CAN BE DOWNLOADED FROM ANY PC.

MAGICAL POWERS ONCE ENTRUSTED TO ONLY A FEW CAN NOW BE BESTOWED UPON YOU AT ONCE!

THE LATEST PSYCHIC TOOLS FROM REV. WILLIAM ALEXANDER ORIBELLO, DRAGONSTAR AND OTHERS

DIVINE BIBLE SPELLS: LIVING A PROSPEROUS AND HAPPY LIFE BY UNDERSTANDING THE SECRETS OF THE HOLY BOOK

There are many secrets in the Bible that you can flourish from – but first you must know where AND HOW to look. Let this work by William Alexander Oribello and Dragonstar operate as your personal guidebook.

YOU'VE HEARD IT SAID A THOUSAND TIMES . . . *WITH GOD ALL THINGS ARE POSSIBLE!* HERE ARE LINKS TO HIDDEN MYSTICAL MEANINGS IN THE BIBLE THAT YOU WERE NEVER TAUGHT IN CHURCH! DISCOVER WHAT ONLY A FEW "TRUTH SEEKERS" REALIZE — THAT A SECRET CODE HAS BEEN EMBEDDED WITHIN THE SCRIPTURES THAT COULD MAKE YOU PROSPEROUS ALMOST OVERNIGHT. Among The Many Things You Will Learn Are: ** Magick and Metaphysics are NOT of the Devil, but were always a major part of Christianity until such teachings were denounced during the Middle Ages. ** That the burning of colored candles at specific times and on specific dates plays a significant role in a program of Biblical illumination that can lead an individual to riches. ** There is a reason why the Three Wise Men arrived in Bethlehem with a variety of types of incense, including Frankincense and Myrrh. Burning incense while repeating certain verses from the Bible can triple the manifestations of your desires. ** That money is NOT the root of all evil, but is our GOD GIVEN right! No one needs to be poor. Abundance is part of the natural flow of God's Universe. TAKE CONTROL OF YOUR LIFE! PUT THESE DIVINE BIBLE SPELLS TO WORK FOR YOU NOW! (Some of this material was originally published in Divine Money Spells).

ORDER: DIVINE BIBLE SPELLS for just $22.00

WANT MORE INFORMATION ON THE SAME TOPIC? - Read the original BIBLE SPELLS as well as CANDLE BURNING WITH THE PSALMS by Wm Oribello. —$22 each – all 3 of these titles - $55.00 + $6 S/H

THE MEDIUMSHIP OF SPIRIT: THE ASCENSION OF WILLIAM ALEXANDER ORIBELLO

Authored by William Alexander Oribello, Abridged by Aurora Thyme, Designed by Tim R. Swartz

AN IMPORTANT SPIRITUAL MESSAGE TO HIS STUDENTS, FRIENDS AND ASSOCIATES — "Though I am in spirit, I am NOT dead! I am still here to assist in your needs."

"It is funny that one really never stops to consider what life is all about until it is over," declares the late metaphysician and occult adept from his new home in the spiritual realm. "We should come to accept help from the Ascended Masters whose mission is to bring the Great Wisdom of God the Creator to Planet Earth and usher us back to the Golden Age of Mankind that has eluded us for so long."

The CONTENTS of this masterful book include: ** LIFE THE GREAT MYSTERY ** RETURNING HOME ** TO YOUR GOOD HEALTH ** LEAVING IT ALL BEHIND ** MAKE YOUR WISHES COME TRUE ** THE CHOICE IS UP TO YOU! ** THE SPIRIT OF ABUNDANCE ** GUIDING OTHERS ALONG THE PATH ** SO YOU WANT TO LIVE FOREVER? ** THOUGHTS MADE REAL ** THOUGHT ENERGY AND HOW TO USE IT ** LISTEN TO WHAT THE UNIVERSE IS TELLING YOU ** FIVE GREAT SECRETS YOU MUST KNOW!

ORDER: THE MEDIUMSHIP OF SPIRIT (Expanded Edition) for just $20.00

WANT TO LEARN MORE ON THIS TOPIC? We highly recommend ( ) THE SEALED MAGICAL BOOK OF MOSES and ( ) SACRED MAGIC REVISED – ADD $20 EACH TO YOUR TOTAL ORDER

TIMOTHY BECKLEY, BOX 753, NEW BRUNSWICK, NJ 08903